977.252 C28

Cathcart, Charlotte, 1877-
1964.

Indianapolis from our old
corner

✓
977.252    Cathcart
CAT        Indianapolis from
           our old corner.

19002

Lewis & Clark Library
Edwardsville, Illinois

RUBY E. DARE LIBRARY
Greenville College
Greenville, IL 62246

D1295436

Meridian Street north from Fourteenth Street

(BASS PHOTO)

977.252
C28

# Indianapolis From Our Old Corner

### by Charlotte Cathcart

Indiana Historical Society

1965

977.252
Cat

LEWIS & CLARK LIBRARY SYSTEM
P. O. BOX 368
EDWARDSVILLE, ILL.  62025

Copyright 1965
by the
Indiana Historical Society

Designed and produced by The Studio Press Inc.

# Indianapolis From Our Old Corner

144176

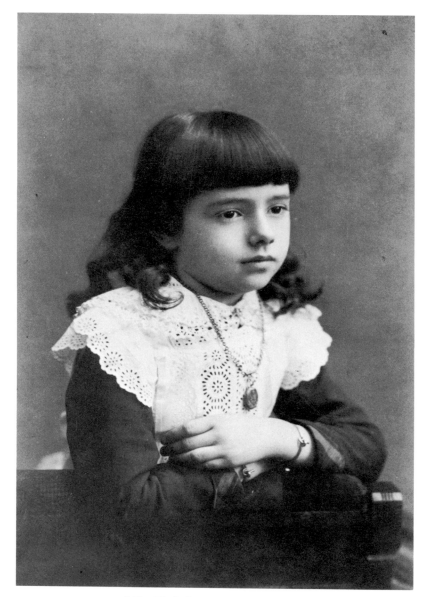

Miss Pink Cathcart, at age seven

# About the Author

In an early disaster Charlotte's doll sustained a broken leg. It was just what happened to a storybook doll in a tale called "Poor Pinky Pet's Dolly." The family began to call her Pinky Pet. Pinky, or Pink, lasted throughout her life: she will always be Pink to those who knew her.

She inherited a memorable personality and predilection against conforming. The Morrises, her mother's maternal ancestors, were imprisoned in Windsor for nonconformance prior to leaving for America in 1619. They followed the frontiers westward through the Carolinas and Pennsylvania during five generations. One of her ancestors who failed to conform in North Carolina was executed in 1692.

The families of Pinky's maternal grandmother go into the England of James I. But those of her great grandfather Robert Morrison and her grandfather Andrew Cathcart stop in the eighteenth century for romantic reasons—both of those young men eloped to America with girls (Ann Irwin and Ellen Weir) who were not forgiven by their families and who in proud retaliation disowned their ancestors.

Such indignation must have been hard for girls if they, like Pink, dearly cherished their parental environment.

ROBERT C. MARTINDALE

# Contents

                    *Page*

Indianapolis as It Was . . . . . . . . . . . . 9
Our Neighborhood . . . . . . . . . . . . 13
The Sewalls and the Girls' Classical School . . . . . . . 20
Pennsylvania Street . . . . . . . . . . . . 23
Meridian Street . . . . . . . . . . . . 27
I Tangle with Lion Cubs . . . . . . . . . . . 29
Downtown . . . . . . . . . . . . . . 30
The Cyclorama Building . . . . . . . . . . . 37
Lighting—Gas and Electricity . . . . . . . . . . 39
Charles Mayer's Store . . . . . . . . . . . 41
Katie's Bicycle Suit . . . . . . . . . . . . 42
Laurie's Store . . . . . . . . . . . . . 44
Doctors . . . . . . . . . . . . . . . 45
State Fair . . . . . . . . . . . . . . 49
Streetcars . . . . . . . . . . . . . . 50
Entertainment and Social Life . . . . . . . . . 53
Society Editor . . . . . . . . . . . . . 64
Groceries . . . . . . . . . . . . . . 67
Papa's Store . . . . . . . . . . . . . . 68
Witness in Court . . . . . . . . . . . . 71
Tennessee Street . . . . . . . . . . . . 72
Christmas . . . . . . . . . . . . . . 73
"Our Old Corner" . . . . . . . . . . . . 79
Base Hospital No. 32 . . . . . . . . . . . 82
Afterward . . . . . . . . . . . . . . 88

## ILLUSTRATIONS

Miss Pink Cathcart, at age seven . . . . . . . . *Frontispiece*
Grace Episcopal Church . . . . . . . . . . . 8

The Transfer Car . . . . . . . . . . . . . . . . 8

Miss Rena Tucker and Miss Kate Cathcart . . . . . . . . 10

The Cathcart Cottage . . . . . . . . . . . . . . . 13

A Picnic at Fairview Park . . . . . . . . . . . . . . 17

Girls' Classical School . . . . . . . . . . . . . . 20

Mrs. May Wright Sewall . . . . . . . . . . . . . . 21

Girls' Classical School Residence . . . . . . . . . . . . 22

"Bobtail" Mule Car . . . . . . . . . . . . . . . . 23

Tinker House . . . . . . . . . . . . . . . . . 24

The Blind Asylum . . . . . . . . . . . . . . . . 26

The Bates House . . . . . . . . . . . . . . . . 31

The New York Store . . . . . . . . . . . . . . . 36

The Cyclorama Building . . . . . . . . . . . . . . 38

Meridian Street south from The Circle . . . . . . . . . 46

The State Fairgrounds . . . . . . . . . . . . . . 48

A Summer Streetcar . . . . . . . . . . . . . . . 52

The When Building . . . . . . . . . . . . . . . 54

Fair Bank Park . . . . . . . . . . . . . . . . . 54

Boathouse and Towpath at Fairview Park . . . . . . . . 57

English's Opera House . . . . . . . . . . . . . . 58

Judge William P. Fishback, Harriet Cleland, the Reverend
    Myron W. Reed, and Jessie Christian . . . . . . . . 59

Towpath and Canal . . . . . . . . . . . . . . . 63

Mother's Cameo Pin . . . . . . . . . . . . . . . 66

Papa's Store . . . . . . . . . . . . . . . . . 69

Katie, at age seven, and Pink, at age five . . . . . . . . 74

The Cathcart Parlor and Sitting Room . . . . . . . . . 76

Miss Kate Cathcart at the piano . . . . . . . . . . . 78

Miss Pink Cathcart sewing in her home . . . . . . . . . 80

The Cathcart Family on the front porch . . . . . . . . . 81

Miss Pink Cathcart at Contrexeville, 1917 . . . . . . . . 86

Grace Episcopal Church

(BASS PHOTO)

The Transfer Car

(BASS PHOTO)

# Indianapolis As It Was

There were no paved streets in Indianapolis and very few sidewalks. What walks there were were almost all of brick, some in diagonal patterns. The only stone walk was on North Street between Meridian and Pennsylvania, in front of the Blind Asylum. Grass grew between the stones.

Practically everyone's property had a fence, either iron or picket, and a rose-covered front porch where the family spent the summer.

The small, mule-drawn streetcars went on Pennsylvania Street only as far as St. Joseph Street, where there was a turntable. The wooden Grace Episcopal Church was on the southeast corner of St. Joe and Pennsylvania streets.

Beautiful maples or elms arched across every street in the city.

There was a Transfer Car on Washington Street in front of Charles Mayer's store and every streetcar stopped there. To transfer from one car to another a passenger got off one car, entered the transfer car at the northwest door, had his transfer ticket punched, went out the southeast door, and got on to the car desired.

The streetcar tickets were five cents, and later were six for a quarter. No charge for transfers.

Meridian Street was paved with cedar blocks as far as Tinker Street. It was the first street in the city to be so treated.

Tenth Street was called Cherry Street, Thirteenth called Home Avenue, and Sixteenth Street was Tinker Street.

Summer streetcars were open cars and had seats with reversible backs so that the cars need not be turned around at the end of the line. A streetcar ride was a great treat on summer evenings.

There were high bicycles and tandems with solid tires.

It was popular to have tintypes made by photographers who came by in a wagon.

Almost every family had a barrel of apples in the basement for winter consumption and a good supply of watermelons in summer.

The ice wagon was a most welcome event. Ice was sold by the pound. Children in the neighborhood begged for chips of ice from the iceman. The larger boys rode on the step and took chips without asking.

Carpets were hung on the clothesline and beaten by the

Miss Rena Tucker and Miss Kate Cathcart attired for
swimming at Lake Wawasee

men of the house, then stretched back into place and tacked down—a truly arduous task.

About the turn of the century cigarettes began to be smoked, but only by the so-called sports of the town. Each package had a photograph of an "actress" of doubtful reputation.

There were no sewers and practically no plumbing in the houses.

A drugstore sold only drugs and perhaps a few cigars, and in the window there was only a large bottle filled with green liquid.

Natural gas was used for heating. There was a large natural-gas flare in front of the When Building on Pennsylvania Street.

Base-burner stoves were used before the coal furnaces that were great boons until they "went out" from clinkers.

The G.A.R. held its parades on Memorial Day and had commemorative services at Crown Hill.

Red woolen underwear was generally worn by both men and women and it was thought dangerous to wear "summer underwear" before May. Women and children wore home-knitted woolen petticoats. We used to recite:

> Under the sod, under the clay,
> Lies Uncle Billy Dan'els,
> Who early in the month of May
> Took off his winter flannels . . . .

Women also wore knee-length, high-necked, elbow-length cotton suits and black cotton stockings, for swimming. They clung tightly when wet. Men wore dark woolen bathing suits, knee-length and with short sleeves. Wide horizontal stripes were fashionable.

For women fashion decreed black cotton stockings, high-buttoned shoes, large bustles, and bangs. Both feet were kept firmly on the floor when sitting.

To be in style, one had to have fretwork in the doorways and arches in his house, and transparencies in the window. Also lambrequins. Everyone had to have a "patent rocker."

There was nearly always some member of the family who played the piano which was usually a square grand. In the evenings when friends came in there would be duets. Everybody sang. All entertainment was homemade —parlor games, puzzles, and reading aloud.

There were no window screens.

If one traveled from town to town, he went by train, with the seats covered with red Pullman plush and cinders as big as peas. There was a water tank at each end of the coach with one glass for everyone to share.

In the summertime, no matter how hot, women wore high-necked, long-sleeved dresses. Men wore heavy black suits and vests, and they kept their coats buttoned tightly in the presence of ladies.

Little girls wore pigtails tied with high bows. Boys up to two years wore dresses.

There were inside shutters.

Every family displayed a red-plush photograph album and school children kept autograph books.

The When Band played every Saturday evening until eight o'clock on the balcony of the When Building which had three floors.

There were three-cent and two-cent pieces in circulation, one-dollar and two-and-one-half-dollar gold pieces. The silver dollar was commoner than paper. One-dollar gold pieces were very small and easy to lose.

Cows roamed the streets and often lay down in the streetcar tracks.

Gentlemen walked to their businesses and a wife would warn: "You had better hurry: Mr. Fishback has gone past. . . ."

Almost everyone knew everyone else.

It cost twenty-five cents to have the grass cut. The head of the family usually cut it himself.

The Cathcart Cottage

Almost every house had a driven well in the back yard. Hand pumps had to be primed in winter.

If a child had a sore throat, his mother put a piece of bacon around his neck, covered it with flannel, and fastened it with a safety pin.

Men wore watch fobs and large watches which had to be wound with a key. The last sound in the house was Papa winding his watch.

After that, there was no sound at night except the barking of a dog.

# Our Neighborhood

Memory is a road down which we can go to any place we have been. I like to go to the corner of Pennsylvania and Pratt (now Ninth) streets in young Indianapolis. On the southeast corner stood a white cottage with a characteristic front porch and white picket fence.

Living there were Robert Weir Cathcart, his wife Alice Morrison Cathcart, and their two-year-old daughter Katie. On June 22 of the year 1877 they were destined to become my father, mother, and sister.

Memory has a way of escaping until suddenly something is fixed in your mind, and from there on it becomes a ready association. The first thing I am sure that I remember is lumber piled beside our cottage. The cottage had been bought by my Grandfather Morrison as a wedding present for my parents in 1870. It was being turned into a three-story house.

Our next-door neighbor was Caleb Newell Lodge. Newell was older than my sister Katie and I and used pretty much to rule the neighborhood. (Later he founded the Lambs Club.) Newell had an uncle, for whom he was named, who was always sending him some sort of gift. Once he sent him a bicycle which you propelled with your feet, it having no pedals. Newell promptly put this in the woodshed. At another time this uncle sent Newell a Rocky Mountain goat and cart. Newell used to charge us pins for a ride with him in the cart to the grocery or around the block.

We had a game in which all the children of the neighborhood joined called "London Bridge is Falling Down." Newell was always head of one side and either Albert Fulton or Elmer Edson, both about Newell's age, head of the other. Each of the rest of us was given a choice of sides after considering the offers of the opposing leaders. Newell always asked something like, "Which would you rather have, a pearl house with emerald shutters or a diamond boat with ruby oars?" Then Elmer would offer: ". . . or a piece of hot gingerbread?" Katie and I nearly always lined up behind Elmer since we knew nothing about diamonds and emeralds, but we did know about gingerbread.

14

Newell would lie on the grass and make poetry about all of us. This was great fun.

Hanford was the oldest of the Edson children. He was very studious. I remember one year his father, Dr. Hanford A. Edson, minister of the Memorial Presbyterian Church, gave Hanford a Geography for Christmas. This made a great impression on all of us.

The Fulton boys were Albert, Rob, and Fred, sons of the Harmon H. Fultons. Rob was to become minister of the Fourth Presbyterian Church. Their parents were nice but quite strict with the boys. One evening all three were sent to bed without supper. Mrs. Edward H. Eldridge who lived next to them was a most sympathetic person and that evening, after she saw Mr. and Mrs. Fulton go out, she made sandwiches and sent them along with some cookies to the boys by means of a string and spool contraption which her daughter Kit and the rest of us had rigged up between the Eldridge house and the Fultons'. I am sure the Fulton boys' parents never learned of this rescue.

Judge and Mrs. Lewis C. Walker lived next door to the Lodges. Their very pretty daughter Camilla was much older than Katie and I and spent her time playing the piano. The Walkers had a yellow horse called Charlie which they treated like a lap dog. One hot summer day Mrs. Walker astonished Nellie Richards (whose family moved into the house where the Fultons had lived) and me by asking if we would like to take Charlie and go for a ride. We were much excited. Mrs. Walker asked if either of us had a watch. Nellie said yes. It was something she had won in a baby show years before and didn't run. But it was a watch. So she said yes. We were to stay out an hour.

Walter Herron, son of Mr. and Mrs. Frederick M. Herron, lived near us. He had built a rowboat but he didn't know how to get it to the canal. Nellie and I thought this was a golden opportunity, so the three of us put the boat in a cart, fastened it to the Walker's buggy, and headed Charlie toward the canal. Walt stood up in the buggy, flourished the whip, a thing which poor Charlie had never seen before, and off we went.

We got the boat to the canal, but poor Charlie was all covered with white foam. Nellie and I were much distressed, but Walt said he knew how to cure the horse.

We drove down to the north side of the Meridian Street Methodist Church, at Meridian and New York streets, where there was a long hitching pole. Walt tied Charlie to the pole, then went into the church and emerged with six large palm-leaf fans. We each took two and fanned Charlie dry. Poor Charlie now looked like something that had come from curling irons. When we returned him, we had been gone almost two hours. Mrs. Walker said nothing, but we were never asked to take another ride.

Nellie Richards' parents were the Edward Richards. Nellie had a sister Bessie who had a marvelous singing voice but she was several years older than we. Nellie however was a beauty. Later Lige Martindale, Judge Elijah B. Martindale's youngest son, fell in love with Nellie and gave her a magnificent ring. In a few days he came back for it and apologized: "I'm afraid I'll have to take that ring, Nellie, Emma's looking for it everywhere." Emma was one of Lige Martindale's elder sisters.

The Charlie W. Smith family lived around the corner from us on Pratt Street. The children were Margaret, Grace, Albert, and Kate. Albert was always getting into trouble or doing something his parents didn't approve of. Yet he did his best, I am sure. One Sunday his Sunday-school teacher asked each child to memorize a saying from the Bible during the following week. Albert promptly forgot about it, but the next Sunday, when called upon, was able to recite an oft-repeated "golden rule" of his parents who were great whist players: "Don't trump your partner's ace."

16

Grace Smith was always up to something. There had been a funeral in the neighborhood which Grace had watched with profound interest. The more she thought of it the more she felt it would be nice if they had a funeral in their family. So she went up to their attic and dug out from an old trunk a black silk dress which had been her grandmother's. This she took downstairs and fastened to the front door. Then she seated herself on the front steps with her face buried in one of her father's handkerchiefs.

Mrs. Smith was sitting at an upstairs window darning stockings. She could not see what went on just below. It was not long before a neighbor came past and seeing the distressing tableau went in by the back door and upstairs to inquire of Mrs. Smith what it meant. Mrs. Smith came down and took Grace into the back yard; there, she later said gravely, she met her own funeral.

The Pratts who lived up the street, had two children, Lois and Ruth. Ruth when quite young was taken to an art exhibit. One of the paintings was titled, "The Kiss of the Siren." Little Ruth was shocked by the Siren's lack of wearing apparel and gave the Siren a good spanking.

A Picnic at Fairview Park

Farther down the block lived the Meigs family. Mr. Charlie Meigs was a great leader of his Sunday school. He said his idea of heaven was one large Sunday school picnic. My sister Katie exclaimed in alarm: "Oh, Mr. Meigs, I didn't know there would be chiggers in heaven!"

The Joseph R. Perrys lived across the street in a little white brick cottage where the Girls' Classical School was later to be, and next to where the Indianapolis Public Library now stands. Mr. Perry was not well but would drag himself to his drugstore on East Washington Street every day. We would ask him how he was and in the most cheerful voice he would say, "Almost dead, thank you."

There were even more children in our neighborhood. There were Will, Luella (whom we called Pudge), and Charlie, children of the William A. Rhodeses. One very cold day Newell Lodge told Pudge that if she touched her tongue to the iron lamp post, it would stick to it. Pudge at once tried it, and found that Newell was right. Our mother and Mrs. Lodge were quickly summoned and freed her in some way while the rest of us were rather hoping they would call the Fire Department.

There were also Mamie, Carrie, and George Denny, children of Caleb S. Denny. The Denny family lived for a time with Mrs. Denny's mother, Mrs. George Lowe, on the northeast corner of Pratt and Meridian streets. They were a great joy to me as they also liked to climb trees. This was not true of Tom, Walter, and Arthur Whallon, children of the Rev. Edward P. Whallon who was minister of the Fourth Presbyterian Church. They lived in the parsonage on Pennsylvania Street.

There were Blanche and Harry Dollens. Harry had a huge Saint Bernard dog which he would hitch to our sled and let him pull us up and down St. Clair Street. If we fell off, the dog would stop and look around, waiting until we were on the sled again.

Then there were the John M. Godown children—

Mary, Lottie, and Kate; the Franklin Landers children—Julia, Pearl, Dwight, and Tommy; the Aquilla Jones family consisting of Charlotte, Rob, and Florence.

There was Newell Lodge's cousin from Chicago, Abby Watson, who often came down for a visit. Abby was great fun and entered into all our games no matter what: hanging on to the back of the "bobtail" streetcars, getting a bucket of water for the iceman's horse in exchange for a piece of ice; climbing trees for cherries; or swinging on the gate.

Older than Katie and I and too dignified to enjoy such fun were Minnie and Florence Coffin, our cousins, daughters of the Dave W. Coffins. Mrs. Coffin was our Aunt Annie, mother's sister. They lived across the street.

Uncle Dave Coffin was a partner in Wiles, Coffin & Company, a wholesale grocery store on South Meridian Street, and a most valuable uncle. We used to go to the store with Florence and Minnie, and Uncle Dave would give us all the roasted peanuts we could carry. Even on Sundays he always found sticks of licorice in his pockets and cut off pieces for us with his penknife. It was delicious.

Minnie and Florence used to give us pieces of beautiful silk, scraps from their dresses, for our doll clothes. Katie could sew a little, but as I was considered too young, my cousin Florence (who was always very kind) would tie a string for me to a pin. It was indeed hard to imagine how the older girls were so skillful . . .

Aunt Annie was an artist. She did china painting, had her own kiln, and fired the china herself. I used to watch her by the hour, and she would often help me paint some small vase or dish. One year Aunt Annie took first prize at the State Fair for a picture she painted, an oil of a bunch of grapes. It was hung upside down but got the prize anyway.

# The Sewalls and the Girls' Classical School

In 1879 Theodore L. Sewall founded the Indianapolis Classical School for Boys. It was first on College Avenue and in 1881 moved to the northwest corner of Alabama and North streets. In 1882 Mrs. Sewall started The Girls' Classical School, located on Pennsylvania Street just north of what is now the Public Library. Mr. Sewall soon gave up the boys' school and he and Mrs. Sewall (known as May Wright Sewall) both served as principals of the new girls' school. As a residence for out-of-town pupils they rented the building which still stands on the southeast corner of Pennsylvania and Walnut streets.

Girls' Classical School

(COURTESY OF THE PROPYLAEUM)

Mrs. May Wright Sewall

The Girls' Classical School became a thriving institution. Mr. Sewall was of medium height and rather slender, dark haired, and kindly. But Mrs. Sewall was a large woman of sturdy carriage. In later days she wore a wig which was never on quite straight and flat-heeled shoes. There was no nonsense about Mrs. Sewall. She used to come into our classroom, and after speaking a few words to Miss Fredonia Allen, she would make a few observations to us, looking through a large magnifying glass which enlarged her eye and made her a Cyclops of most forbidding appearance.

The kindergarten and intermediate classes were held on the second floor of the school, Miss Corinna Robbins teaching the former and Miss Allen the latter. On the ground floor were the advanced pupils with Miss Marie L. Bright and Miss Elizabeth Hughes as teachers. Miss Belle Bronk was the French teacher and a Frenchwoman. Miss Emily Bingham taught elocution.

Girls' Classical School Residence

Among the pupils in my class were Kate Sullivan
(who became Mrs. John E. Hollett, Sr.), Dolly Van-
Camp (Mrs. John T. Martindale), Nell Baker (Mrs.
Chandler Dallam), Carrie Burford (Mrs. Henry Rose
Danner), Louisa Fletcher (Mrs. Willard Connelly),
Florence Heywood, Adelaide Fairbanks, daughter of
the Vice-President, Myla Coburn (Mrs. Frank Ferry
Powell), Mamie Ransdell (Mrs. Richard Warner),
Julia Fletcher (Mrs. J. Alfred Barnard), and Kate Chaf-
fee of Kansas City.

Mrs. (Dr.) Pauline Morton was instructor of gym-
nastics. The gymnasium was on the top floor and was well
equipped with rings on which one could swing to the ceiling and see as far as Delaware Street.

Mr. Sewall died in 1895 and Mrs. Sewall continued
the school for a few years. We forgot Xenophon easily,

but not Mrs. Sewall. The Caroline Scott Harrison Chapter of the D.A.R. later occupied the school building.

# Pennsylvania Street

Pennsylvania Street from Tinker (now Sixteenth) Street to Ohio Street was lined with lovely maples which reached clear across the street. Almost everyone came to Pennsylvania Street to walk, no matter if they lived on Delaware or Meridian. College Avenue had horse cars but on Pennsylvania we had mules. The cars were excellent to steal a ride for a few feet. This was done by the Fulton boys, Albert, Rob, Fred; Newell Lodge, Bert Wood, Elmer Edson (his brother Hanford was always studying), Albert Smith, Grace Smith, Katie, and me. And even Tom Whallon whose father was minister of the old Fourth Church. This lovely little church was on the

"Bobtail" Mule Car

(BASS PHOTO)

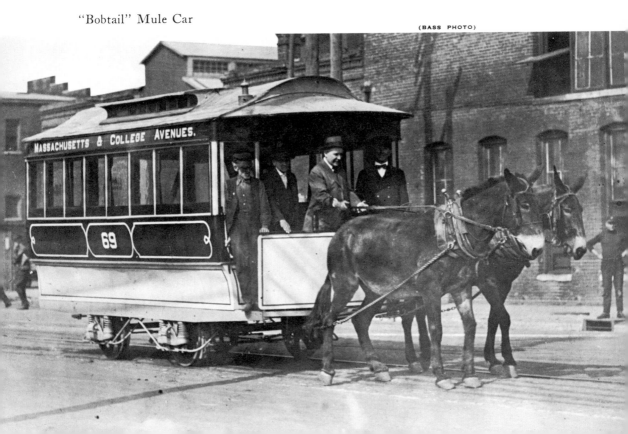

Tinker House, First Home of the John Herron Art Museum,
at Talbot and Tinker (now Sixteenth) Streets

(BASS PHOTO)

northwest corner of Pennsylvania and Pratt streets, on the
back of the lot where the Plaza Apartments now stand. It
was red brick covered with ivy and there we had, under
the nine walnut trees, all our strawberry socials with
Chinese lanterns.

In Pennsylvania Street many gentlemen wore silk hats
and all carried gold-headed canes. I used to make chains
out of catalpa flowers in season and present them to these
staid gentlemen who duly put them around their hats. It
was a friendly world and a child could walk all over town
in perfect safety.

Pennsylvania Street was a street of homes. There were
very few handsome residences compared with Meridian
Street, but Pennsylvania with its shady maples, its frame
houses with picket fences, its little black mules pulling
"bobtail" streetcars with accommodating drivers, was
most pleasant for pedestrians. Those who walked downtown were sure of meeting friends on Pennsylvania
Street.

As it was not paved, in winter after a heavy snow or
after a spring thaw Pennsylvania Street was almost im-

24

possible to cross. But in summer its brick sidewalks, pleasant street lamps, and carefully tended lawns provided an attractive route downtown. The streetcars seemed to go far north when extended from St. Joe to Tinker Street.

When Katie and I were growing up the families who lived on Pennsylvania Street were well known if not so affluent as those on Meridian Street. Theodore C. Steele lived in a brick house where the Art Museum now stands. Hugh H. Hanna, Major William J. Richards, William H. Coburn, Albert Baker, Chapin Foster, O. G. Pfaff, Hervey Bates, Jr., Caleb S. Denny, J. K. Lilly, and John Johnston had homes there, and also Henry Schurmann, the Rev. Joseph S. Jenckes, Jr., Ferdinand Winter, the Tarkingtons (parents of Booth), and Jacob Cox the artist; also Edward H. Mayo, James M. Bradshaw, Dr. John N. Hurty, Hanford A. Edson, Robert W. Cathcart, David W. Coffin, James I. Lodge, Judge Lewis C. Walker, William Conner, James A. Wildman (Mr. Wildman was postmaster), Charles D. Meigs, Franklin Landers, Max Leckner, Judge James B. Black, Charles Krauss, and James H. Baldwin.

There was the Blind Asylum—the Indiana Institute for the Education of the Blind—on the north side of North Street between Meridian and Pennsylvania with its pretty park, Pomroy's Drugstore, the homes of the James L. Fugates and John C. News, and the Indianapolis High School.

There was also University Park and residence and office of Dr. Joseph Stillson, and residences of John H. Murphy, Judge Joseph E. McDonald, Charles B. Cones, William H. Morrison, and John S. Spann.

There was the Baptist Church on the northeast corner at New York, the First Presbyterian Church on the southwest corner at New York, the Second Presbyterian on the northwest corner at Vermont, and the houses and offices of Dr. Franklin W. Hays, Dr. John M. Kitchen, Drs. John

C. and Isaac Walker, Carl Fisher's bicycle school, and Dr. Hurty's drugstore with Sam, his big Maltese cat, always in the window. At the southwest corner at Ohio there were the school board's quarters with the Public Library in the rear; Brennecke's Dancing School in the Vajen Block, the Denison Hotel, Dickson's Grand Opera House, Paul Krauss's haberdashery, and the office of Hannah E. and Lucius W. Moses, opticians. I fear I may have forgotten some. . . .

The Blind Asylum

(BASS PHOTO)

# Meridian Street

Beyond the nine great walnut trees of the Fourth Presbyterian Church a venturesome child would come upon Meridian Street with its handsome residences, spacious lawns, ornate iron fences, brick sidewalks, and cedar-block paving. On Meridian Street there were expensive carriages, Victorias with well-groomed horses, polished brass, and shining harness. The ladies who rode in them carried parasols, wore high-necked flowing dresses, feathers and plumes, kid gloves, and smiles. The coachmen were aloof and proud.

The gentlemen in Meridian Street seemed to favor Prince Alberts, cutaways, or box coats, watch fobs, gold-headed canes, and silk or derby hats. In winter some wore fur collars. What would they have thought of men today wearing *bracelet* watches?

The mansions of Meridian Street seemed much too far apart for children to call back and forth to one another. There were also many great churches which, with the exception of Christ Episcopal on the Circle at Meridian, have all disappeared. And who would have thought that the vast and permanent-looking Blind Asylum with its high iron fence and park with grazing cows, would ever be removed?

A big apple orchard on the southeast corner at Tinker Street ended Meridian Street.

It would be impossible to mention all the well-known families of that period on North Meridian Street. But I recall a few whom we knew in the eighties and nineties.

Meridian Street began, for us, at the Circle where the Monument was then being built to honor Indiana's soldiers and sailors. During construction there was a high wooden fence surrounding it and horse-drawn "moving" wagons were backed against it waiting to be rented.

On the southwest quadrant of the Circle was a small frame cottage in which lived Mrs. Charles W. (Abby) Cady and her small grandchildren, Kitty, Charlie, and Blake Stone. Also on the Circle was English's Opera House and the residence of William H. English and his family. Mr. English was a friend of our grandfather, John I. Morrison. His grandson Willoughby Walling sometimes came to visit him and always made us a number of calls.

The Circle Park Hotel was on the southeast section of the Circle and on the northeast the residence of William H. Morrison. On the corner of the northeast section stood, as it does today, beautiful Christ Church. In the southwest segment there had been a small church called "Wesley Chapel." Mrs. O. G. Pfaff told me in 1964 that she was christened at Wesley Chapel in 1864—the year she was born. The structure was remodeled and became the Sentinel Building.

On the southeast corner of Ohio and Meridian streets was the Pyle House, a rambling frame hotel with rather narrow entrance. There were always several old men sitting in front of it on "Captain" chairs, all smoking pipes. On the block above Ohio Street, on the east side, was the Third Ward School, and on the corner, Plymouth Congregational Church.

Across the street, at the southwest corner of New York and Meridian, was the Meridian Street Methodist Church with its two beautiful spires, and also in that block the home of Mr. John H. Vajen and family.

On the east side above New York, University Park was as it is today with the exception that there was a small wooden bandstand in the center, where the When Band sometimes played, and more and bigger trees.

Across the street were the homes of Dr. Edward F. Hodges, Edward F. Claypool, and Frederick Fahnley. The Isaiah Mansur house was on the northeast corner of

28

Vermont and Meridian streets. Also in that block were the Allen M. Fletchers, W. J. Hollidays, and E. B. Martindales. The Blacherne, one of the earlier apartment houses, was not then built.

Above Michigan Street lived Alfred Harrison and Brainard Rorison. Above North Street on the east was the Blind Asylum and its park reaching to St. Clair Street. On the west side were the George W. Sloans, Edward G. Corneliuses, John F. Wallicks, Louis Hollwegs, and north of them the John H. Hollidays, Daniel P. Erwins, Clarence Wulsins, Joseph P. Wigginses, Col. Eli Lillys, and Addison C. Harrises; also the Henry Severins, Henry D. Pierces, Arthur Jordans, William P. Herods, Charles Mayers, Elias C. Atkinses, and Henry Knippenbergs. And on the corner of Meridian and what is now Sixteenth there was the large apple orchard.

Our mother had a school friend who lived so very far out in the country that it was a rare event when we were able to see her. She lived with her family on their farm at what is now Thirtieth Street. She was Mrs. Abby King.

At this time all the land above Fall Creek was pasture, orchard, and farmland.


# I Tangle With Lion Cubs


Dr. and Mrs. Franklin W. Hays lived in the north side of a double white brick house on the southeast corner of Pennsylvania and New York streets. Mrs. Hays was an expert telegrapher and Dr. Hays an able and popular physician. They had two lion cubs. I have always liked cats and thought it would be such fun to pat a real lion.

One day Dr. Hays was exercising the two lion cubs and had just crossed New York Street in front of the Baptist Church. I thought this was my golden opportunity and asked if I might pat them. Dr. Hays said the lions would be delighted to continue their walk up the street, with me between them. We set off and I soon was ready to tickle the ear of one. He evidently thought I intended to play. He jumped up on me with such force that he knocked me over on to the other lion. He, too, felt this was going to be a romp and the first thing I knew I was on the sidewalk with two lions on top of me. They now seemed fairly good size. Dr. Hays untangled us. I regretfully decided that such pleasure as patting a lion was the privilege of a professional trainer.

# Downtown

On the northwest corner of Washington and Illinois streets, presently the site of the Claypool Hotel, was the Bates House, built by Hervey Bates, Sr. His son Hervey, Jr., was our uncle, having married our father's sister Charlotte. It was with great glee that my sister and I, when we were still quite little, would go and spend the day there. There was a "well" surrounded by balustrades on each floor over which one could look from the top floor clear down to the dining room. We seldom got to go into the glamorous public dining room, because our aunt and uncle had a private one in their apartment in the hotel.

I remember our father telling of going down to the Bates House to hear President-elect Lincoln speak. Hervey Bates, Sr., invited my father—then a boy—and his friend Andy Graydon to join the family on the hotel's balcony that day. The boys had each bought a package of twenty-five blank calling cards. They handed these to Mr. Lincoln and asked him to write his name on one for each of them. Instead Mr. Lincoln signed all the fifty cards. I still have one of these cards.

(BASS PHOTO)

The Bates House

Across the street on the northeast corner of Illinois and
Washington streets was the Claypool Block. A few doors
east of it was Lieber's art store. There could never be a
more delightful place to go as Mr. Lieber and his four
cordial sons, Otto, Carl, Robert, and Herman, were always there. Our aunt, Mrs. D. W. Coffin, who painted
china and porcelain, bought her china at Schrader's but
always went to Lieber's for brushes and paint. It made no
difference how small the purchase, we were always shown
the new paintings exhibited on the second floor. In all
these years Lieber's never changed. It would be hard to
find a more delightful person than Mr. Carl Lieber.

The book and stationery store of Merrill, Hubbard and
Company (Col. Samuel Merrill, William H. Hubbard,

and Charles D. Meigs) had been located on the south side of Washington Street east of Meridian. Samuel Merrill was colonel of the Seventieth Indiana Volunteers of which Benjamin Harrison was general during the Civil War. My father enlisted in this regiment when he was seventeen and became a sergeant. After Colonel Merrill died, his son Charlie became a partner in the Bowen-Merrill bookstore which moved to the north side of Washington Street and became Bowen-Merrill Company, predecessor of the Bobbs-Merrill Company. It was there that the disastrous fire occurred in which so many firemen perished under falling walls. The company rebuilt on the south side of Washington Street and H. P. Wasson & Company built on the former location.

One day our mother was in H. P. Wasson's store. Mr. Wasson told her he had just bought a few kitchen stoves and was quite distressed as he doubted if they would sell. Then he related several other things in the store about which he worried. Our mother suggested the store seemed to be a burden and that he could easily retire. Why didn't he? He said:—"Well Alice, just the minute I am worth $20,000 I intend to." At the time most people thought this far in the distance, a forlorn hope.

On the north side of Washington Street next to Bowen-Merrill's was William Haerle's store. One was always met by Mr. Haerle or his son George. I can see the store as clearly as if it were here today. Their stock was women's accessories such as fancy collars, laces, embroideries, and some gloves. There was a wire running above the counters on which was hung a most attractive assortment of these. Ladies never made a mistake when buying at Mr. Haerle's.

Next to Haerle's was a trunk store. It was called "The Bee Hive." Across Meridian Street to the east was the tobacco store of Charles F. Meyer & Brother, and next to it was Frederick M. Herron's jewelry store where Mr.

Herron and his popular son Fred held forth. I well remember Mr. Herron used to help me up onto a chair and let me see and even try on rings which were in an open tray. On one of these occasions when I was five years of age, Mr. Herron said to me: "You know what I am going to do? The next time I get married I am going to marry you!" I had no idea what he was proposing but was deeply convinced it was a threat of some sort most undesirable. I scrambled down from the chair I was standing on and ran into our father's store and clutched my father. He tried to convince me that Mr. Herron was only joking and that what he intended was meant as a compliment. Nevertheless, it was months before I could be induced to enter Mr. Herron's store again, even when accompanied by either of my parents. I was sure that he would carry out his threat.

Our store, Cathcart, Cleland & Company, bookstore, came next and then Craig's candy store. The latter was always an attraction and usually filled with customers.

Then came Tucker's glove store with Mr. Hannibal S. Tucker and Miss Sullivan behind the counters. I remember how we used to sit on a high stool and rest our elbows on a velvet cushion while Miss Sullivan would laboriously fit a pair of gloves on us. How many must have been ruined! But Mr. Tucker sold only gloves and seemed to have an infinite supply of them.

Next to Tucker's was Bingham & Walk's jewelry store. Later, it became Julius C. Walk & Son. They had a big clock out on the sidewalk painted black and gold. Above it, it said "Walk's." One day it stopped. Mr. Charlie Walker went in and said:

"I notice your clock outside says 'Walk's.' Does it ever run?"

I do not remember what was between Walk's and S. A. Fletcher & Company, bankers, where the Washington Hotel now stands. My sister and I had a breath-taking experience at the bank. It was summer and our plum tree had an unusually heavy bearing. Mrs. Hanford Edson, who lived across the street from us on Pennsylvania Street, said she would pay Katie and me $1.25 for a bushel of plums. Our father helped us pick a bushel and Mrs. Edson paid us with a check instead of cash. We had never seen such a thing but our father took us down to his store and had us endorse the check made out to Katie and Arlie Cathcart—I was sometimes called "Arlie" in those days. There were a number of customers in our store and our father asked one of them if he would take us with him to the bank. He wrote a note to Stoughton J. Fletcher explaining that we were his daughters.

The gentleman took us to the door of the bank and told us to ask for Mr. Fletcher. I shall never forget the chill which we experienced in such a forbidding place. No shelves with books, jewelry, dry goods, or anything to look at! A bare floor and bare walls!

We saw in front of us a very elegantly dressed person whom we took to be Mr. Fletcher. My sister who was seven (I five) addressed him. He informed us that he was a guard and told us where to find Mr. Fletcher.

We went to Mr. Fletcher who read our father's note and called in a very loud voice, "Wocher, I say Wocher!"

A nice young man came forward and Mr. Fletcher said: "These are Bob Cathcart's kids, give them whatever they want."

Mr. Wocher, one of the Wocher brothers, took charge of us and eventually we received our $1.25. No bandits ever made quicker escape from a bank than we two small children did from Mr. Fletcher's.

Around the corner on Pennsylvania Street was Krauss's haberdashery. I was never in it but it had one of the windows where we used to stop when we played the window game that I shall explain later.

On the other side of the street, on the southeast corner of

34

Market and Pennsylvania streets, was the old post office. It was there that the "Knights of the Golden Circle" held their meetings during the Civil War, or at least smuggled their ammunition. It was always a post office until taken over by the American National Bank founded by John Perrin in 1901. We were older then and took much interest in the new bank, as Mrs. Perrin was our cousin, Eleanor Bates Perrin, whom we always thought remarkably attractive.

Farther up the street was the Baldwin music store where the Wulsins worked, and Mr. Brennecke's dancing class which all of us attended. It was on the second floor of the Vajen Block. On the corner of Pennsylvania and Ohio streets were the public school offices and back of them in the same building the public library where Miss Nancy Baker (later Mrs. Evans Woollen), Miss Florence Baker (Mrs. Jacquelin S. Holliday), Miss Eliza Browning, and Miss Isabella C. Schonacker were the librarians.

On Ohio between Pennsylvania and Meridian streets was "Doctors Row." The Denison Hotel was on the southeast corner of Pennsylvania and Ohio and next to it was the Grand Opera House owned and managed by George A. Dickson and Henry M. Talbott.

Charles Mayer's wonderful store (more about it later) was on the south side of Washington Street between Illinois and Meridian. West of it was the L. S. Ayres store and east of it was Albert Gall's which offered carpet, oil cloths, wall paper, and window shades.

On the southwest corner of Meridian and Washington streets was the Indiana Banking Company. Later the Merchants National Bank was on this corner. Across Meridian Street there was the Eastman, Schleicher and Lee's store which offered carpets, draperies, wall paper, etc. Then came the popular New York Store and P. Gramling & Son, tailors. Above Gramling's was the abode of Simon Yandes. Tall, slender, and (as I remember him) white haired, Mr. Yandes was one of Indianapolis' great characters. He looked as if he had stepped right out of Dickens. He was a kindly retiring man whom but few ever knew. He came across the street to our father's bookstore frequently. One day he asked our father to bring some books over to him and I went along. I shall never forget his front room, the only one we saw. It was large and square and completely filled with newspapers. They were even on the window sills and on the mantel of the red stone fireplace. There was a large table in the middle of the room and it, too, was stacked with old newspapers. They were heaped and piled everywhere so that

The New York Store

(BASS PHOTO)

only Charles Dickens could have done justice to the extraordinary scene.

Beyond this was Browning and Sloan's drugstore. It was 100 per cent drugstore, no suggestion of department store as today. I shall never forget their severe window. It was draped in dark green velvet and had nothing in the foreground but the druggist's fancy bottle about three feet tall, containing a mysterious green liquid. The mystery of that bottle has remained in my memory all these years, whereas the windows of today's drugstores have such a variety of things that the old saying proves true: one cannot see the wood for the trees. Robert Browning, the druggist, lived at 700 North Meridian Street and George Sloan on the northwest corner of North and Meridian streets.

# The Cyclorama Building

The Cyclorama Building was on the north side of Market Street just west of Illinois. It was circular in shape and contained life-sized paintings of the Battle of Gettysburg. They were very realistic. After one had been there once one could hardly bear to go again. So evidently it did not pay and soon was taken over by Bostock's Zoo.

Bostock's was well patronized though I never remember a crowd. Around the edge were cages for small animals, monkeys, and some of the big cats. In the corner a large circular cage housed animals which performed. Under it was a pit for the bears.

It was some time before the Bostocks discovered what was making the lions so furious most of the time when performing. They were expected to sit around the edge of the cage and their tails hung outside and over the edge, in easy reach of the bears. The bears saw these waving objects and would reach out and grab them and then

The Cyclorama Building

(BASS PHOTO)

chew them. Wire fencing had to be placed all around the lower edges of the performing cage to discourage this game.

Once the manager allowed my sister and me to hold a basket containing three new-born leopards. I never felt anything so soft as their fur.

Evidently the Zoo did not pay either for it was not long before the building became a sort of garage where the first owners of electric automobiles recharged them. Hervey Bates and Fred Ayres were among the first to have such cars. We also had an electric which would go nearly fifteen miles an hour when newly charged. It was thought a great speed.

However, it was not long before the old Cyclorama Building was razed and the Traction Terminal Station was built in its place. It became a busy spot, with interurban passengers coming and going with the new sense of hurry that accompanied motor vehicles.

38

# Lighting—Gas and Electricity

I do not remember when there were only oil lamps for lighting, except in the small towns and in the country. In the seventies and eighties homes in Indianapolis were lighted by gas. There were chandeliers in the center of the rooms and wall brackets with arms for side lights. We had, and I think most people had, fancy oil lamps on center tables for reading.

On some of the side lights we had what were called "Welsbach burners." These were very fragile mantles which would fall apart if touched, but they gave out a white light, whereas the usual gas flame gave a more yellow light. If someone stood at a side bracket and turned on the gas at the very moment another person dragged his feet across the carpet and touched the gas burner, the gas would light. The electric spark thus made forecast the electricity that would come.

Everyone had a lighter for the high center light. These lighters were small metal rods about a yard in length with a gadget on one end to be used in turning on the light key and a branch bracket on the other which held a yellow wick. One first turned the key, then applied the lighted wick to the burner. There was always a slight smell of burning tallow accompanying this operation.

Streets were lighted by gas. There were iron posts at every corner and at the alleys, which supported large glass lanterns. Young men came with small wooden ladders and kerosene lighters and lighted them at dusk. These lamplighters were faithful in all sorts of weather. In winter we used to have them come in to get warm at the base-burner stove in our library.

In 1888 two cousins, Daniel W. Marmon and Charles C. Perry, organized the Marmon-Perry Light Company and started furnishing the city with electricity for lights.

Mrs. Caroline Marmon Fesler, Mr. Marmon's daughter, told me her father put up the $5,000 needed for them to get started. They experimented with lighting with electricity in a workshop back of the William H. Morrison home next door to Christ Church on the Circle. After a while they had bought out all the other electric light companies in town and formed the Indianapolis Light and Power Company.

The old Charles W. Cady cottage in the southwest section of the Circle served as the office of the company from 1892 to 1897, and then the cottage was torn down and the Journal Building erected on the site, and the Light and Power Company moved into the new building. The company did not have very many employees, and I used to go down and address the envelopes for the bills by hand. There were but a few hundred then.

Thomas A. Wynne was one of the officers of the company, and Minnie Watterson, who was to become Mrs. Wynne, made her home with us for twelve years. Mr. Wynne wanted to do something nice for Miss Watterson and had an electric light installed in her room. But the light was so bright we had to put on dark glasses when sewing there. Mr. Wynne soon installed a less bright light. (We always called Minnie Watterson "Uncle Billy" because of her daring, so "early in the month of May. . . .")

The first electric street lights were carbon arc lights and did much sputtering. But soon all homes and businesses were using electricity, and the streets were lighted with it. I remember when the electric lights were turned on, on Pennsylvania Street. We were excited and wondered how we could stand such brilliance. Mr. and Mrs. Charles Perry and their sons Jim and Norman came to our house frequently. The light in front of our house made such a glare that Mr. Perry had a black spot painted on the globe so as to cast a shadow on the porch.

# Charles Mayer's Store

To go downtown without a visit to Charles Mayer's was a wasted trip. It was both a store and a sort of museum where one could go and admire beautiful objects. Few of us can remember Charles Mayer, Sr., but his two welcoming, hearty sons, Charles and Ferd, were always there, never deserting a small customer for one of more substantial means.

To step into Charles Mayer's was like entering another world. Silver to the right, silver to the left, jewelry to the front, all looking like it had just been polished, and everything in excellent taste.

To the right were sterling trays, plates, flat silver, and every other conceivable article for the table. Near the elevator on the same side were picture frames in silver and leather. On the left aisle there were clocks, barometers, and watches, and farther back one found fancy scarves and handbags of all descriptions.

China and glassware were upstairs, beautiful pieces imported from all over the world.

But the real wonderland of childhood was Charles Mayer's toy department. It was Santa Claus' storehouse open twelve months of the year. Appropriately, it was on the top floor. Going up in the open, ironwork elevator one could see all the glittering ware attractive to grownups, while anticipating the child's world to come. For the girls there were dolls, dolls, dolls, from every corner of the globe. They were of all sizes and races and costumes. There were also doll houses and doll trunks fitted out ready for a trip through the looking glass with Alice.

Next to the dolls were music boxes with tiny chickens and ducks on top waltzing around to the music. There were Christmas trees that folded up and fragile Christmas ornaments such as one had never seen.

On the other side were the toys for boys. Miniature replicas of every mechanism of that day: old-fashioned locomotives, fire engines—the entire fire department in red helmets with horses at full speed. There were soldiers in red coats, blue coats, and gray coats, and officers, too. There were famous regiments in military regalia, calvary and infantry and lancers, waiting for the command from some small hand. There were balls of all sizes and for all purposes, pop guns, express wagons, tops, toy cannon, and, beyond the elevator, hobby horses on the dead run, white, gray, bay, dapple, each ready for the bridle of Santa Claus.

At the back was a separate department of children's furniture and vehicles: wagons big enough to ride in, and brightly painted wooden imitations of locomotives with steam domes and whistle domes and bells that rang warnings to adults.

One wonders now, "Was there ever actually such a store as Charles Mayer's?"

# Katie's Bicycle Suit

It was about 1885 that the first "safety" bicycles came into use. Before that there had been the "high" bicycle which it was more painful to fall off of. But the regular "small-wheel" bicycle established itself in short order. Ellis Hunter may have had the first and I think Carl Fisher had the second. In a very short time Carl started his bicycle school on North Pennsylvania Street on the west side between New York and Ohio streets where there had been a skating rink. To learn to ride a bicycle one took lessons from a qualified professional like Carl.

Winifred Hunter had one of the first women's bicycles and my sister and I got ours soon after. These were heavy affairs with solid rubber tires. When I think how strenuously we used to ride out to Broad Ripple along the canal towpath to enjoy a chicken dinner at Mrs. Brennermann's, and then ride home immediately afterwards, and on those solid tires, I am amazed we did not collapse. At least we got no punctures.

At all events we had our bicycles at the cost of $75.00. This was quite a sum for such frivolity in those days and our dear father tried to convince us that our savings were of more value. But we wanted bicycles.

After getting them, my sister Katie felt she should have a bicycle suit, so she and I went down to Besten and Langen's to see what they had. They were located on the south side of Washington Street a few shops west of Pennsylvania.

There were only two bicycle suits in stock as there was not yet much demand for them. One was very plain but we thought the other very beautiful—brown, with a satin-lined jacket, bloomers, and a pleated skirt. Katie looked lovely in it. But it cost $15.00—way beyond our reach.

While we were looking longingly at the suit, the clerk asked us how much money we had. Katie emptied her purse which contained $8.00 and a few odd cents. My small hand purse had but a handkerchief as its contents. After consultation with Mr. Besten, the clerk came back to say we could have the suit for $8.00. Of course, we were overjoyed.

But when we reached home and related our experience to our parents, they were far from delighted at our accepting this charity. Our father insisted upon returning the suit the following morning. But Mr. Besten insisted that they had not lost money on the suit and in turn persuaded our father to take it back to Katie. He agreed but gave them $2.00 more, they arguing that $10.00 was more than ample. So the bicycle suit was returned to a joyous Katie.

Of course, for a long while after that all our family conscientiously bought their clothing at Besten and Langen's. Even our aunt, Mrs. David Coffin, and her daughters Minnie and Florence, went there to shop. Mr. Besten came over to our father's store and said that Katie's bicycle suit was the best advertising they ever had.

# Laurie's Store

William Laurie & Company was a dry goods store on the east side of Meridian Street just south of the Circle, where the Electric Building now stands. It was a big store with large double front doors and two long aisles. It was the best place to buy medium-priced embroideries and some summer yard goods such as percale. At the back of the store were blankets, linings, pillows, and linen.

Mr. Laurie was a tall, white-haired, very erect Scotsman who never conversed with his customers. The clerks were very agreeable young women. There were high stools for the clerks to sit on and chairs for the customers. This was also true of other stores at that time. But Laurie's animating feature was a brightly nickled overhead railway connecting all the counters with the cash desk. The cables ran constantly, with a clacking that anticipated purchases—efficiently acknowledged. When you bought your calico, your money was put into a little car and went whizzing away across the ceiling. The change came back almost immediately, the car banging into the proper siding at your counter. In many stores of that day the clerk who took payment must call out, "Cash Girl!"—and that person would come and make change. It was more exciting at Mr. Laurie's.

One day my mother needed another yard of embroidered flouncing to sew on to a petticoat and went in to Laurie's to get it. Barnum and Bailey's Circus was in town that week and mother wanted to make her

44

purchase and return home before the circus parade would cut across her path at Ohio and Pennsylvania streets. She could hear the steam calliope approaching in the distance.

There was not one clerk in the entire store, yet all the doors were open and Mr. Laurie himself was in the rear. My mother went up to him and asked, "Mr. Laurie, isn't there someone who can wait on me?" He replied, "Yes, madam, just as soon as the young ladies return from watching the parade."

The clerks had taken their high stools to stand on, and were already established on Washington Street watching for the elephants. There was nothing for my mother to do but join them and watch, too.

# Doctors

There were about two hundred physicians in Indianapolis in the eighties. At that time the north side of Ohio Street between Meridian and Pennsylvania streets was called "Doctor's Row." The doctors who had offices there included Fernandez O. Clemmer, George W. Combs, Joshua A. Compton, Henry Jameson, Patrick H. Jameson, A. S. McMurray, Allison Maxwell, Luther L. Todd, J. M. Tomlinson, G. W. Vernon. Across the street were the offices of Dr. George Hasty and Dr. Ernest A. Wehrman.

There were, of course, many leading physicians who were located elsewhere. Dr. Joseph Eastman had built a sanatorium on the corner of Delaware and Vermont streets. It was he who began to use what is called a "wick" in abdominal surgery, as a drainage. This is now used, I am told, all over the world. Dr. T. B. Harvey had offices at Pennsylvania and North streets. He was the preceptor of Dr. Orange G. Pfaff. Later Dr. Horace R. Allen built

Meridian Street south from The Circle, with Mr. Laurie's
Store on the left

(BASS PHOTO

46

47

the National Surgical Institute at Capitol and Ohio streets. Almost every physician had his loyal followers who considered him the best in Indianapolis or, quite probably, the best in the world.

I remember when I was in France during the First World War with Base Hospital No. 32, hearing some of the pranks that these doctors used to play on one another.

In 1887 there were in Indianapolis

    eight nurses

    one pharmaceutical manufacturer, Eli Lilly and Company, on East McCarty Street

    three oculists: John W. Culbertson, James L. Thompson, and Daniel W. Thompson

    five opticians: William T. Marcy, James N. Mayhew, Hannah E. Moses, Joseph Harry, and Mayer Steinberg

    thirty dentists.

There were no hospitals as we know them today.

The State Fairgrounds

(BASS PHOTO)

# State Fair

The old State Fairgrounds was located on what was later called Morton Place. It extended north from Nineteenth Street to Twenty-second Street between Delaware and New Jersey. During the Civil War the Fairgrounds was used as a training and then a prison camp and called Camp Morton.

To get to the Fair we took a Pennsylvania streetcar downtown and transferred at the old Transfer Car on Washington Street in front of Charles Mayer's store, to an Alabama streetcar. The main entrance to the Fair was on Alabama Street at Nineteenth. In front of the three large gates a man was always selling balloons. Most children were made happy with a red one which was tied to the wrist by a string, or around a finger. There were three buildings on the grounds, all frame. The main building was the length of a city block and had two floors with a wide stairway from the first to the second. Long, narrow windows extended the entire height of the main floor and its balcony. On the main floor were displayed carriages and buggies, handsomely painted. The Baldwin Piano Company had its display in the center on a platform about three feet high surrounded by a fence made of wooden slats and covered with a bright carpet. Here Belle L. Closser played a piano against a background noise of lowing or protesting farm animals. It was the only music at the Fair. Around the walls were shelves displaying bottles of fertilizers, prize grains, seeds, and cereals. A child spent little time admiring these.

The balcony of the main building was given over to the Fair office and to stalls for display of items of interest to women. In the office five men and one woman (our aunt, Maria M. Finch, widow of H. Byron Finch) kept all the records and were paid $100 for the week's work

—then considered a fabulous pay. In the stalls were such things as spreads, tablecloths and napkins, paintings, pies, jellies, cakes, and preserves.

There were large doors at the north end leading to the other two buildings. One contained horses, cattle, sheep, pigs, hens, and ducks. All looked well fed and groomed for the occasion. The other building was given over to farm machinery. Larger threshing machines were displayed under tents decorated with brightly colored streamers.

If families took lunch to the fair, it was eaten out in the grass and rain was a catastrophe. The mud was so deep one even dispensed with seeing the outside displays.

Although the Fair was the big event of the year, I don't remember that it ever seemed crowded. During Fair week the Denison Hotel was always full. Judge E. B. Martindale owned the hotel and his entire family stayed there. One day there were not enough tables to seat the State Fair visitors, and two young country girls were asked to sit at the Martindales' private table. During one of the meat courses one of the girls reached far over and put her biscuit upside down in the steak juice, saying to her sister: "Sop in the gravy, Sal, Paw pays as much as anyone."

# Streetcars

The first streetcars, which were called "bobtails," had five windows on each side and a small step at the rear. In the winter straw was spread on the floor to keep the passengers' feet dry, and the drivers, who rode outside, wore long bearskin coats. Later, there were iron stoves in the cars, which passengers who felt cold would sometimes stoke with more coal. The small black mules had a difficult time when the cars would slide off the track, as they often did in icy weather.

50

Pennsylvania Street had but one track with a side switch at the Blind Asylum at North Street. The line terminated at St. Joe Street with a turntable in front of the small, frame Grace Episcopal Church.

The fare throughout the city being five cents, the driver would frequently count the number of passengers to see if it tallied with the number of nickels deposited in the glass container at the front of the car. Mrs. Evans Woollen, Sr., when she was still Miss Nancy Baker, worked in the Indianapolis Public Library at the corner of Pennsylvania and Ohio streets. She told me that one day she was riding to work on the Pennsylvania car and had on a new blue suit. After the driver had stopped and counted the passengers and the nickels, he said, "The young lady in the blue suit put in a button instead of a nickel." Miss Nancy paid her nickel but the glory of her new suit was gone.

The little streetcar mules all had names, and our Uncle Frank Morrison used to be startled into wakefulness each morning by a passing driver calling out loudly, "Git up Frank!"

It was no unusual thing for stray cows to lie down across the track and refuse to budge. On one occasion when the car was thus stopped near our house our father, who was sitting on our porch, thought of a scheme to save the day. He cut a watermelon in two, let the cow sniff it, and put half of it in the gutter. The cow decided to give up its place in favor of the melon and the car moved on its way.

The drivers were always most friendly and accommodating. They would often advise a lady passenger: "You'd better bring your umbrella, it's going to rain." They would then wait until she ran back and got her umbrella. At Christmas time they always helped passengers laden with packages to be mailed at the old post office on the southeast corner of Market and Pennsylvania streets.

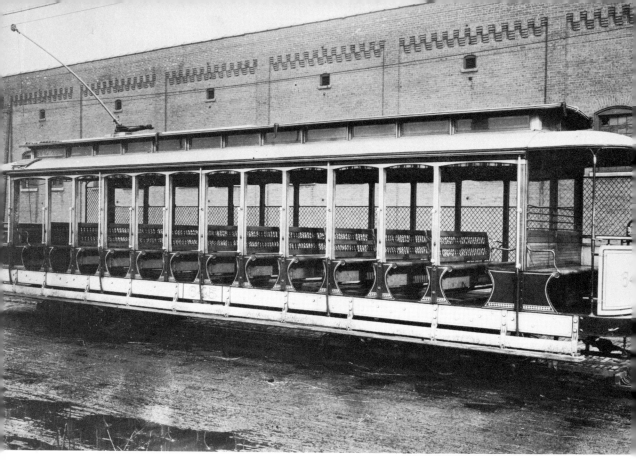

A Summer Streetcar

But the real thrill came when Indianapolis got electricity and trolley cars began running. At first, the trolley was forever coming off the overhead wire and the conductor would have a dreadful time getting it on again. One now had to wait at the corner for the car to stop instead of in front of his own house. The old Transfer Car went out of existence.

Many people were confused about the source of electricity for the new cars and rumor spread that it was dangerous, now, to step on the track rails. An elderly aunt of ours asked the conductor about this. He reassured her: "No madame, it is dangerous only if you put your other foot on the trolley . . ."

The special summer cars, open, with rows of seats like pews across the width of the car, had a running board on the side along which the conductor swung collecting fares while grabbing the brass handles to support himself. All

52

young persons envied the conductor this remarkable skill.

The summer cars were a great boon to many of us who stayed in town all summer, for we could pay a five-cent fare on the Pennsylvania car, and get a transfer to the Illinois car which would take us to Fairview Park. We then paid five cents to return and got another transfer which took us as far as Irvington. Another five cents would bring us home on Pennsylvania Street. By the time the hot evening passed, we had cooled off. All for 15 cents.

Parties were given on chartered summer cars. The cost of a car for such an evening was under $10.00 and the car could go anywhere in town, on any track. I remember one evening our cousins Minnie and Florence Coffin gave such a party. All the guests assembled at the Coffins. Romeo Johnson stopped for my sister and me and the three of us walked up to pick up Booth Tarkington who lived on Pennsylvania Street two blocks above us.

After our cooling streetcar ride we returned to the Coffin's for refreshment and entertainment. The girls had a game in which fifty or more small objects were placed on the dining-room table and the guests were given three minutes to inspect the articles. Then they turned their backs on the table and listed on a slip of paper all the objects they could remember. Booth had the longest list and won the prize. On our way home he confessed he had put down anything that had come into his mind, and as only the number of articles were counted, no one discovered that most of the articles he listed were not on the table.

# Entertainment and Social Life

Although every Saturday night during summer the When Band used to play on the balcony of the When

The When Building

(BASS PHOTO)

Fair Bank Park, present site of St. Vincent's Hospital

(BASS PHOTO)

Building, there were also band concerts in University Park. While there was never a great crowd, the concerts were always well attended. There were no seats and never any disorder. The band played loudly so that talking by young people was not frowned upon.

John Philip Sousa and his band often came to Indianapolis, playing in Tomlinson Hall. Sousa always wore a white uniform trimmed with gold braid.

During the summer there were also outdoor plays. I remember "Hiawatha" being presented in Fairview Park. Tiers of seats were put on the hill on the east side of the Canal and the play was given on the west side. This was quite an event for Indianapolis.

There were also open-air concerts at Fair Bank, a park on Illinois Street where St. Vincent's Hospital now stands.

Indianapolis counted a large number of Germans in its population and they were responsible for some of the city's best musical offerings. There were the Maennerchor and the German House concerts, attended by members and invited guests.

The ladies of the town all had their days "at home," when they served tea to guests. Invitations to these were the hostess's calling card with the date of the "open house" engraved thereon.

There was much calling in those days. Men, both young and old, made formal Sunday calls. I recall one Sunday afternoon there were twenty-five young men at our house at the same time. Sometimes Alvin Schmidt and Fritz Krull would bring their violins and my sister or mother would accompany them while they played. Those who could (and those who couldn't) would join in singing.

New Year's Day was quite an event. Several ladies would join together and hold "open house" at one of their homes. A list of "open houses" would be published in the papers the day before. Then the number of gentleman callers would even reach a hundred. Punch was served.

The large cut-glass punch bowls were presided over by daughters of the hostesses. The young men came with top hats and canes and all the callers wore heavy overcoats and overshoes. Some would have umbrellas. In looking back, I wonder where all the overcoats and overshoes were put in average hallways, and how each man found his own when he was ready to leave.

Young men used to serenade the girls in summer. And during the winter holidays boys home from college would rent a hall and give a dance.

There were card parties and card clubs. Euchre and whist were the chief games. Our parents belonged to three card clubs of twenty-four members each. Each club met once a month. Each couple donated a sum toward the purchase of prizes, one for a man and one for a lady. The prizes usually cost about $2.50. The weather never prevented attendance, although most couples came on foot. When our mother and father returned home, we would always call downstairs and ask: "Did you win the prize?" It seems to me they always said yes.

The churches provided the greatest part of our entertainment, including suppers, socials, and fairs. The most popular events were summer picnics. Sometimes we went on "express" wagons pulled by two horses hired for the occasion. Or we might go by train to some nearby place of interest. These picnics meant a tremendous amount of work on the part of the ladies of the church, for they prepared all the cold fried chicken, baked ham, jelly and cheese sandwiches, chicken salad, potato salad, cakes, and a variety of pies. Seldom were there tables, so cloths were spread on the grass. And there were always linen, not paper, napkins.

One summer Frederick A. W. Davis, one of the officers

56

Boathouse and Towpath at Fairview Park

(BASS PHOTO)

of the Water Company, took the picnickers out to Golden Hill by flatboat on the Canal. It was a novel adventure. We boarded the boat at about Pratt Street. Horses pulled us out and back. The voyage took all day.

Lemonade was the chief drink on these excursions and it was pretty flat without ice. There were no paper cups; tin cups served the purpose. Everyone always had a wonderful time, and returned home tired, with many "chiggers."

The Fourth Presbyterian Church, at Pennsylvania and Pratt streets, held a strawberry social every summer.

English's Opera House

(BASS PHOTO)

Tables were set up under the huge walnut trees and the spacious lawn was lit with Japanese lanterns. This, to a child, was truly fairyland.

There were literary clubs in which our mother read numerous papers, and, of course, theaters. There was English's and there was the Grand Opera House owned and managed by George Dickson and Henry Talbott. Less important plays usually went to the Park Theatre. I saw Booth in *Hamlet* when I was almost too young to comprehend it. But mother read the play to Katie and me and said that even if we didn't understand it, we would always know that we had seen the greatest actor in the greatest play.

The Indianapolis Literary Club and the Gentlemen's Club held their meetings at Plymouth Church, a red-brick building on the southeast corner of Meridian and New York streets. Most of the literary lights who visited our city lectured there. These included Dr. Matthew Arnold who was the guest of Mr. and Mrs. William P. Fishback. The lecture was in the Congregation Room on the second floor and for some reason our parents and Mr. and Mrs. Cleland were late. They were met by the two McCulloch boys, David and Carleton (later Dr. Carleton) who acted as ushers and cautioned them to enter very quietly: "Shuss. . . the audience is asleep. . . ."

Once at the Literary Club Mr. Fishback shrewdly argued in debate with the two eminent lawyers, Albert

Judge William P. Fishback, Harriet Cleland, the Reverend Myron W. Reed, and Jessie Christian

Beveridge and John L. Griffiths and won on a standing vote for having proven his case. At this there was some acclaim which Mr. Fishback acknowledged. "I hope," he added, "that no one here believes for a moment that I agree with anything I said."

One of the most outstanding entertainments of the year was the Flower Mission Fair. The Flower Mission was a charitable organization that raised money each year by holding a fair in Tomlinson Hall. Several members would join together and buy space for a booth which they would then decorate to represent a Swiss chalet, a French cafe, an English cottage, a German beer garden (where only coffee and soft drinks were served), or a log cabin. Those in attendance wore appropriate costumes. Candies, cakes, pies, preserves, knitted pieces, hand-painted china, embroideries, and even antiques were sold.

During the evening home-talent entertainment was provided. I remember how our lovely cousin Mamie Ransdell danced the Highland Fling dressed in Scottish costume at one fair, and Marie Rich sang "Over Hill and Dale" at another. Dancing would follow, with Henry Hart and his two daughters usually playing the new waltzes.

In the early nineties William P. Fishback conducted a small class in Shakespeare. Its members were my sister Katie (who became Mrs. Clarence Martindale), Hattie Cleland (Mrs. John A. Blair), Jessie Christian (Mrs. Demarchus Brown), Fanny Fugate (Mrs. G. Harold Noyes), Father Joseph Chartrand, Almus Ruddell, Ed Raub, and Bob Fishback. They met once a month, and also sometimes took trips to nearby places of interest. Myron Reed, pastor of the Second Presbyterian Church, and Jim Riley sometimes joined them.

One summer Mrs. James H. Ruddell, mother of Almus and Frank, invited the class to their house in Allisonville for a chicken dinner. As neither Father Chartrand nor

Jessie Christian rode bicycles, Frank Ruddell and I were invited to fill in. There had been no rain for several weeks and the dust was very thick. However, we made it and were at dinner having a wonderful time, when suddenly there was a tremendous clap of thunder followed by a downpour of rain.

The storm was too severe for us to consider returning to Indianapolis and Mrs. Ruddell invited us all to spend the night. There was no telephone, and the great question was how to let our parents know we were all right. At Noblesville there was a telegraph station, and Bob Fishback and Almus Ruddell volunteered to hitch up Almus' horse and buggy and go there and send messages to our families. This eased our minds, though we dreaded having the boys start out in such a rainstorm.

In the morning the sun was out, but the mud was deep. We decided to follow the nearest route which would take us along the towpath on the canal. The path was very muddy and slippery. We were almost opposite the site of the Woodstock Club when Fanny Fugate got too near the edge of the canal. The ground was soft and gave way and she went into the canal—bicycle and all.

Bob Fishback was after her in a flash and they both climbed out with our help, soaked to the skin. All of us were covered with mud.

We remembered passing a house about a mile back, and hurried there. The woman was ironing. She took us in despite our appearance and was most kind. Bob Fishback insisted he liked being in wet clothing after the heat of the last weeks, so the boys rode home. We girls waited until they sent a hack from Horace Wood's livery stable to take us home. By the time it arrived Fanny was dry and her clothes had been pressed.

The Fishbacks did much entertaining in their home. Twice a month they gave a dinner party and if there was any celebrity in town, he or she would be invited. These dinners were no small affairs. Twenty or more guests would be seated at table and an elaborate dinner was always served. Other guests were invited to come in afterwards. Our family was often there, and met such theatrical personalities as Nat Goodwin, Richard Mansfield, and E. H. Sothern.

Jim Riley was usually there and was always accommodating in reciting his verse or telling an amusing story. Other frequent guests were Louis and Carrie Howland, Mr. and Mrs. Augustus L. Mason, Mr. and Mrs. John L. Griffiths, and Mr. and Mrs. Alfred Potts.

Entertainment was provided by the guests. Charades were particularly popular, and if there were visiting actors or actresses present, or members of the stock company playing a season at the Grand, they would join in.

One Sunday evening Richard Mansfield was among the guests. Wine was served and my sister and I (our parents were not present) pretended we had had too much of it. We were sufficiently convincing that Mr. Fishback asked Mr. Mansfield if he would escort us home. He was staying at the Denison Hotel and our home was on his way. As soon as we were on the sidewalk, we told Mr. Mansfield we were only pretending. He, of course, knew this and showed us how we could have put on a more entertaining act. It was great fun. We never tried it again, but it was something to be coached by Richard Mansfield. . . .

Amateur theatricals were popular, including presentations of Gilbert and Sullivan operettas. I recall a performance of *Patience* in which Lynn Martindale played the "Colonel" and Will Talbott the "Duke," but said the *Journal*: ". . . there were many others who added grace and beauty to the occasion." The Martindales, all of whom had pleasant voices, wore out several scores of the delightful light opera *Robin Hood*.

Towpath and Canal

(BASS PHOTO)

# Society Editor

My sister Kate got a job on the Indianapolis *News* drawing fashion pictures and writing the Woman's Page. One afternoon she came home in high spirits. The paper had offered her a job for the summer as Society Editor, but since she was already working, she couldn't take it, and they asked her to recommend someone. She said, "My sister could take it."

I was only fifteen and I was horrified. I knew nothing about writing or newspaper work. My sister simply advised, "Now NEVER say YOU CAN'T." My parents left it up to me, and the $65.00 the job offered loomed large. It seemed like turning down Providence to refuse.

The next morning when I set out, my sister admonished me:—"Now remember: WHATEVER they ask you to do, say you CAN."

The night before we had attended a party and since we had lived in town all our lives and knew almost everyone and what they were doing, my list of society items was already quite long. Enough to fill two columns at least. I was directed to report to the City Editor, and I shall never forget him. He seemed most kind. After a friendly greeting he asked:

"Do you use a typewriter?" I had never touched one, but I remembered what my sister had insisted, so I said, "Oh yes."

"Well," he said, "you'll find one in the little room across the hall which will be yours for the summer."

I timidly entered the room but saw no machine. I leaned on the table. Up sprang a typewriter!

Somehow I got a sheet of paper into it, and punched a key, but nothing showed. I didn't realize that the ribbon was worn out. I managed in some way to get the roller off and carried it to the City Editor. He looked at it and asked, "What is it?" I replied, "The thing you ink on the typewriter." He smiled.

"Oh yes," he said, "I see. All right, I'll have it inked for you, but it will take some time. Meanwhile, why don't you use a pencil? Your handwriting is good. You have enough items to last several days. Pick out the ones you think best for today and bring them to me when you have finished writing them. It's really very easy."

I went back and wrote like mad.

When I took them in to him, he said, "That's fine. Now why don't you go down to some of the stores and walk around. You may pick up some other items you can use later."

And so it went all summer; the roller never appeared, and in a couple of months I had earned $65.00!

Meanwhile, I had seen a "breast pin" in Charles Mayer's jewelry department. It was a cameo with Queen Elizabeth carved in white on a black onyx setting surrounded by small pearls. This I wanted as a birthday present for my mother, and I wanted it more than I had ever wanted anything.

. It would take all my $65.00.

Mr. Mayer had put it aside for me, and now I was able to go in and claim it.

Ferd Mayer was truly distressed that I was going to put all my hard-earned money on one present and urged me to select something else. But when he found I was adamant, that nothing else "looked like my mother," he reduced the price to $50.00, put the pin in the prettiest box he had, and with a serious expression escorted me to the door. He said very forcefully that I should tell my mother how he felt and that she could exchange the pin for something else if she agreed with him, and he knew that she would.

Mother's Cameo Pin

When I gave mother her present, she was even more emphatic than Mr. Ferd and insisted that I return it. Finally they both realized what it meant to me, and she kept it. I never regretted it, because she continued to wear it throughout the rest of her long life.

# Groceries

There were almost five hundred groceries in Indianapolis in the eighties. These were very different from the ones today; even very different from the small neighborhood store of today. I remember J. T. Powers' store on North Pennsylvania just south of Market Street. It and A. C. Kuhn's on the southeast corner of Illinois and Market streets were the two groceries downtown. These and Buschmann's at Fort Wayne and Cherry (now Tenth) streets were bigger than those in the residential neighborhoods. Railsback's I remember most vividly for it was the one our family patronized. It was on the southeast corner of Illinois and Pratt streets.

I remember the gunny or burlap sacks that lined the south wall filled with beans, onions, potatoes, and dried fruits—apricots and prunes. There was also a barrel of dill pickles from which you fished out what you wanted. If the barrel was less than half full, you almost fell into it spearing a pickle. Then there were two barrels with spigots: one of molasses and one of cider vinegar. Coffee beans were kept in a big sack and sugar in a big tin container. Apples and crackers were kept in barrels, too.

Bread cost five cents a loaf, and one of our neighbors with a large family bought six loaves for a quarter.

At the back of Railsback's store was the butcher shop, divided from the rest of the store by double doors with glass panes. The butcher cut meat on a large block made from the trunk of a big tree and often had a bandaged thumb. Mr. Railsback cut meat and also sold groceries. He wore a big white apron and nearly always gave children who came into his store an apple or stick of candy.

One day a young lion escaped from a small circus showing on a lot across Illinois Street and jumped through the grocery window scattering the customers like an explosion. The lion took refuge under a large ice chest and was finally coaxed back to captivity without casualty.

# Papa's Store

Our bookstore was No. 26 East Washington Street. Never could there have been better-equipped persons to have a bookstore than Robert Cathcart and John E. Cleland. Both loved books, were widely read, and universally liked. When our father was very young, he worked as a messenger boy in Col. Samuel Merrill's bookstore, and when he and John Cleland lay desperately ill, side by side, in an old smokehouse at Pilot Knob, Tennessee, during the Civil War, they agreed that if they ever recovered and reached home they would open a bookstore.

Their shop had the quiet, relaxed atmosphere which attracts men of learning. Men would drop in, some to read, others to find the latest magazines or just to meet friends. Someone was always meeting someone else at Cathcart and Cleland's.

I remember seeing there regularly Judge Addison L. Roache, a handsome elderly gentleman who always wore a silk hat, and in winter a fur cape with high-standing collar. There were also John M. Butler, Gen. Thomas A. Morris, John C. New, William P. Fishback, Charles W. Smith and his partner John S. Duncan, Myron W. Reed, Simon and George Yandes, Oscar McCulloch, Dr. Alembert Brayton, and others. There were younger men: James Whitcomb Riley, J. K. Lilly, and John L. Griffiths. Whenever a new volume of Riley's was published, he would write a verse in a copy and give it to my sister and me.

68

"Papa's Store," the Cathcart and Cleland Bookstore
"Papa" at the left and Mr. Cleland in the foreground

For us children the store was a fairyland, with *St. Nicholas* and the *Youth's Companion*. On the shelves was Hoffmann's "Slovenly Peter" hobnobbing with Miss Kate Greenaway's aristocratic children and the little men and women of Louisa M. Alcott. There were the English publications, beautifully illustrated, where "Old Crummels lay dead in his grave below," and hundreds of other real people like Little Nell, Lady Deadlock, Mr. Pickwick, David Copperfield, Nancy Sikes and her terrible brother Bill, and Whisker the pony.

Then there were the cases of Waterman penpoints, beautiful lace-paper and silk-fringed Christmas cards. And the cover of *Harper's Monthly* with cupids sporting amid bubbles.

Women came into the store also, but not so often as men. Among the frequent visitors were Mrs. W. W. Woollen, Eliza Hendricks, and Anna Nicholas.

I remember a woman who came in once. She said that she loved to read, particularly Shakespeare, and wanted something of his. Our father asked which play she wanted, and she didn't seem to know. He asked if she had read this or that play. She said yes. When he suggested *Romeo and Juliet* she replied: "Well, I have read Romeo, and am just finishing Juliet." My father said that this nearly finished him, too.

I remember that Mr. Fishback, who was dean of the Indiana Law School, asked us once to fill in the names on the school diplomas with fancy lettering. Our mother did the real copperplate embellishments of birds and flourishes for us very expertly. My sister and I did the so-called fill-ins.

Years after the store was closed, J. K. Lilly told me that when he was a young man without much money, he was most anxious to own a three-volume set of ancient history, handsomely bound, which was priced at $15.00. He said our father told him he had read this history and felt that it was inferior to another covering the same period and much less expensive. Mr. Lilly bought this less expensive set and never forgot the incident.

Every other Saturday night the store was kept open until 8:30. Our mother would take my sister and me downtown on those nights and we would all walk home together. Our father had a game which we played: He and my sister would walk in front of my mother and me. They would stop at every shop window and pick out the most unattractive article they could see, saying that was to be either my mother's or my Christmas present. We, in turn, would choose the worst we could find for them. It was lots of fun. To this day when I look into a shop window the first thing I look for is something I could not be induced to possess.

# Witness In Court

My mother and I had been invited out to dinner. Knowing that there would be no time to dress after banking hours (I was working in the Fletcher Bank at the time), I dressed in my best bib and tucker in the morning. This has some bearing on the case.

In the afternoon Frank Wocher, one of the bank's officials, said that I was wanted at the Court House to testify to the soundness of mind of one of our old neighbors, recently deceased, whose will was being contested. Mr. Wocher went with me. I had never been in court before and observed with considerable interest the judge, the jury, and the dilapidated appearance of the courtroom.

When my turn came and the judge asked me to take the stand, I thought this meant to stand up, which I did. When I had been properly sworn and seated, the judge asked how long I had known this woman. I answered for as long as I could remember. He then asked if I would prove to the jury that I knew Pennsylvania Street. I asked where on Pennsylvania Street he wished me to begin. He said anywhere that I might choose.

I started at Washington Street and advanced up the east side of Pennsylvania, recalling every business and building and residence from there to Tinker Street, now Sixteenth Street. Above that all was pasture and orchards. The jury's interest was aroused when I reached Massachusetts Avenue and described the small frame house which had stood where the K-of-P Building now stands, and mentioned streetcars running no farther north than St. Joseph Street.

When I got up to Tinker Street I asked if this was sufficient or should I proceed down on the west side. The jury foreman spoke up and said, "Yes." So down I went, naming every business, building, and residence as far as Ohio Street. By this time I was getting a little tired, and glancing at my watch discovered it was late. I said, "I am sorry but I cannot stay any longer as I have to help get out a financial report before the bank closes for the day."

The Judge looked somewhat surprised, but smiled and thanked me for my testimony which he said had been sufficiently convincing. There was one more question: Would I describe how Miss X, the deceased, had dressed. I replied, "Oh, about the way I do now." Mr. Wocher and I then left.

Later the lawyer for the contestants told me that this was the answer which turned the verdict against him, as one of his strongest points had been that anyone would know by looking at the way Miss X dressed that she was crazy.

# Tennessee Street

Tennessee Street was the widest street in the city. It had no streetcars and in winter was the center of sleigh racing. In the summer it enjoyed the shade of beautiful maples. At the extreme north limit of the street was the Indianapolis Baseball Park where the Methodist Hospital now stands. It was one of the first popular residential streets on Indianapolis' "new north side," and when the State House was built was renamed Capitol Avenue.

With help of the excellent memory of Mrs. O. G. Pfaff and Miss Katrina Fertig I can tell a little about Tennessee Street in its earliest days. Mrs. Pfaff's grandfather, E. H. Alvey, bought property on Tennessee Street in the year 1830 and built his home there. It was called "Alvey's Folly" as it was so inaccessibly out in the country. It was on Tennessee at what is now Tenth Street.

Following the Civil War Tennessee Street underwent a great period of popularity. Our grandfather, John I. Morrison, then treasurer of state, moved to the southwest corner of Tennessee and North streets. Others who lived there included: John D. Howland, William and Robert Haueisen, Judge E. B. Martindale, Col. Eli Lilly, his son Josiah K. Lilly, Governor Albert G. Porter, William Kothe, Alexander Metzger, George A. Reisner, William Coughlen, Judge Roscoe O. Hawkins, Samuel Fletcher, Mayor Thomas L. Sullivan, Andrew J. McIntosh, Dr. Louis Burckhardt, John Rauch, August M. Kuhn, Col. Daniel M. Ransdell, Henry H. Hornbrook, Senator Harry S. New, and Mayor Thomas Taggart. George A. Reisner, Jr., became the world-famous Egyptologist and archaeologist. Col. Ransdell moved to Washington where he became sergeant-at-arms of the United States Senate.

# Christmas

For days before Christmas our kitchen was a place of frantic activity, a good deal of which was devoted to making mince meat. The big porcelain-lined iron kettle was brought out to cook it in. The old tin safe with its perforated door bulged with good things. The "Iron King" stove roared at full draught. The cast iron pestle and mortar were readied to powder spices. Apples which had been stored since harvest time in the cellar were brought up to be peeled and chopped. We children cracked nuts, using a flatiron turned upside down on our laps and a hammer. There were also raisins to be seeded.

In the evenings corn was popped over the coals in the parlor fireplace and strung along with cranberries as Christmas-tree decorations. Silver paper stars cut out by our mother and walnuts wrapped in silver paper also served as trimmings.

Katie, at age seven, and Pink, at age five

My sister and I hemstitched handkerchiefs for our parents' presents. It seemed very hard because the threads kept getting into knots and we had to work in our own room so our parents could not see what we were doing. All presents had to be a surprise.

On Christmas morning our father was up long before the crack of dawn, getting the house warm for the rest of us. This responsibility fell to the fathers of most households and Christmas was no exception. There was the furnace and the old base-burner stove to shake down, the kitchen stove to relight. Mothers meanwhile helped children into warm but voluminous clothing: ankle-length underwear, flannel petticoats, woolen stockings, and woolen dresses with countless buttons up the back. As one looks back on the truly difficult and uncomfortable tasks that our parents daily undertook to make life comfortable for us, it seems almost impossible. Our father would call upstairs:

"Twelve below zero!"—To us it meant only our sleds and perhaps a ride in our uncle's sleigh. But I used often to reflect with satisfaction that if hungry bears attacked us from behind the snowdrifts they could not eat us: they would choke on all the clothes we wore.

My sister and I were awake shortly after our father, peeking with glee at the contents of our Christmas stockings which had been hung from our beds by Santa Claus during the night. The stockings always contained an orange, an apple, a gaudy tin horn, a small doll or two, and other mysterious and unexpected articles. We bounced with excitement, and after getting to the bottom of the stockings, we gathered up our clothes and ran through the hall and down the stairs to the sitting room where we dressed in the warm glow of the old base burner stove.

Our mother, who had sat up late the night before, putting finishing touches to our presents, was ready, too, and came to button us up. In very cold weather our underwear was even fleece-lined and over it we wore muslin drawers edged in crochet made by our mother or "Auntie," Mrs. H. Byron Finch. And our woolen petticoats might also have scalloped edges. Then came a muslin one with even more crocheting, and only finally the high-necked woolen dress which buttoned up the back. Handiwork of our mother.

As soon as we were dressed, we ran into the parlor to

The Cathcart Parlor and Sitting Room

look at, but not touch, the piles of tissue-wrapped presents on and under the Steinway grand piano. One Christmas I had written asking Santa for a hobbyhorse, and I was sure that I could see one camouflaged under our grandmother's big gray shawl. I was also almost sure that it was for me, for my sister did not want even a live horse or pony, and my aunts and uncles certainly wouldn't want it. Yet I couldn't be positive it was mine, and it was hard not to "snoop," but that would not have been fair. So we could only look and dance about until we were persuaded into the breakfast room where our father said the blessing, giving thanks for all the many and special blessings of that day. We then tried to eat our breakfast but excitement prevented. When this was understood we were allowed back into the parlor. But not to touch. . . .

The floor was covered with a grain carpet. There was fretwork in the arches and pretty lace curtains covered the two full-length plate-glass windows. The piano where our attention was centered sat in the alcove built especially for it with leaded, stained-glass windows on either side. There was a marble mantel over a grate fireplace with mirrors above, and in front of this stood the Christmas tree, gay with its silver trimming and strings of popcorn and cranberries.

Finally came the time for opening presents. First there was my old doll Anna who for some days had been missing. She reappeared in a beautiful new dress and real bonnet. Then the shawl (big enough for a horse cloth) was removed, and to my great joy the hobbyhorse! "For Pink from Mamma and Papa." I seemed to have all that life could offer. I called him Prince after my Uncle David Coffin's horse across the street.

Soon the Coffins came, Uncle David, Aunt Annie, Minnie and Florence, crossing through the snowdrifts from their house, bringing their gifts for us in baskets. "Christmas gift! Christmas gift!" they cried.

Miss Kate Cathcart at the piano "in the alcove built
especially for it"

Our gifts for them and theirs for us were placed on the
large dinner table at the appropriate places. The over-
flow was placed on the chairs. Dinner was long delayed
while we all opened packages. Then our uncle said the
blessing and carved the turkey. He was very good-
humored.

There was merriment, singing, and laughter all afternoon and evening. My sister and I bubbled with joy. For
supper there were mince or pumpkin pies and big jugs of

cider. By nine o'clock we could no longer keep our eyes open. We said our prayers and were tucked into bed, hugging our favorite dolls. May everyone recall such a completely happy day. . . .

# "Our Old Corner"

When Indianapolis was laid out, the place in which we lived was spoken of in the City Directory as "439 North Pennsylvania . . . the limit of the city line." That line became Pratt Street and, very much later, Ninth Street, and the house was renumbered 839. Calvin Fletcher was the first owner of the property. He built two cottages on it for his sons Albert and Ingram.

But Albert soon built and moved into a handsome house even farther north (presently 1121 North Pennsylvania Street), while Ingram moved to Meridian Street, where now stands the Antlers Hotel. The cottages were then acquired by the sons of John S. Spann: Thomas and John M. They also soon followed the northward trend: to Delaware Street, north of Twelfth Street.

It seems interesting now a hundred years later that those who moved north moved such a little way: less than half a mile. But men still walked into town to their businesses each morning, just as we children walked to school. Many walked a mile and did so four times a day.

When in 1870 our grandfather gave one of the Spann cottages to his youngest daughter (our mother) and her husband as a wedding present, that was the last change of name in the title. When our father died in 1909, my mother had the present apartment house built on the site. It has been called "The Cathcart" for over fifty years, but I am the last of that name.

Everyone in those days was sure that Indianapolis would move northward and indeed it seems almost to have moved away.

Miss Pink Cathcart sewing in her home

80

The Cathcart family on the front porch—Mama, Papa,
Katie, and Pink

# Base Hospital No. 32

As Indianapolis moves away from "our Old Corner" at the former city limit I do not come to the end of my memory so much as I fear to try my friends' patience. A little later in my life I was privileged to belong to an Indianapolis organization which retained its friendly character under sometimes vexing circumstances abroad. This was Base Hospital No. 32, not far behind our lines in France in 1917 and 1918.

It was in February, 1917, when German and American relations became strained, that several Indianapolis physicians offered to organize some sort of hospital relief in the event that war was declared. It was: April 6, 1917.

The generosity of J. K. Lilly made this Indianapolis project possible. He offered to equip a base hospital and give the sum of $25,000 with the request that the hospital be named after Col. Eli Lilly, his father, who had served in the Civil War. This gift met ready response from our leading physicians and the hospital was soon well on its way. Many trained nurses also offered their services. These were gratefully accepted. Among those who helped organize the hospital were Dr. John Oliver, Dr. David Ross, Dr. Frank Morrison, and Dr. O. G. Pfaff.

Everyone was talking of the Lilly Base Hospital and everyone in Indianapolis seemed to want to help in any way possible. Miss Florence J. Martin was chosen chief nurse. She was a neighbor of ours and she, together with several of the doctors we knew, urged me to become a member of the staff. So I went down to see Dr. John Oliver, the director, who then had his office on the southwest corner of Delaware and Michigan streets.

On my way I met Mary Herod who said that she had just come from Dr. Oliver's and he had told her there was not a corner left for anybody. Mary was a French scholar and seemed to me unusually qualified but I decided to go on down anyway.

After Dr. Oliver's patients had all left, I introduced myself and stated my errand. He asked me what I knew of hospitals and I told him honestly I had never been in any, except for three brief visits, in my entire life. He asked what I knew about nursing and I had to admit I knew nothing. We both laughed and he asked what I did know that might be of service. I said:

"Well, I am a good scrubber."

Whereupon he said: "Well, that is just what we need, so from now on you can count yourself on the hospital staff."

Later, through the efforts of Dr. Carleton B. McCulloch, Mary Herod was also accepted as a civilian employee. I was assigned as secretary to Dr. Edmund D. Clark who was one of Indiana's leading surgeons.

There were two hundred doctors and enlisted men, fifty-seven nurses, and six of us who began as "civilians." Three months later Lilly Base Hospital had been designated an Army unit, Base Hospital No. 32. On September 7, 1917, the nurses took their oath and underwent indoctrination training at Hoboken and Ellis Island.

On October 27 the civilian employees also reported for mobilization. We were now in the Army: Mary Bostwick, stenographer; Georgia Finlay, of Oneida, Illinois, dietician; Geraldine Frost, of Washington, D.C., stenographer; Mary Beaty Herod, interpreter; Gertrude Steffen, stenographer; and myself, Charlotte Cathcart, stenographer. We had quite a farewell at the Union Station and left for Ellis Island to join the nurses. We were there until December 4.

I had never been in a sleeping room since a small child with anyone but myself, and when I entered a large room on Ellis Island with sixty-seven other girls I was somewhat dismayed. We all ate at the same time and on the way to mess we had to pass a barbed-wire fence enclosing German prisoners who looked pathetic.

I will never forget, nor will any of the nurses, the extreme kindness of the soldiers and personnel of Ellis Island. They even held up the ship until the last mail had been distributed. We embarked on the old *George Washington,* which had been converted to a transport, at 10:00 P.M. on December 4. None had the slightest idea what our destination was to be. We had no convoy.

There were on board 750 officers, 8,000 troops, about 1,200 in the crew. The officers included six major generals. There were sixty-seven women.

I think Dr. Carl McCulloch's verses describe the voyage better than anything I could write:


## LINES DEDICATED TO THE BAY OF BISCAY

The terrorizing Teuton and the wily Magyar horde,
Were threatening the Universe and so we went aboard,
That steady transport, *Washington,* one sunny day serene,
To sail the Bay of Biscay in the Fall of Seventeen.

Our sailing was auspicious as we slipped away at night.
They corked up all the funnels and doused every vagrant light,
As we slipped away to Europe with water, wind and steam
To sail the Bay of Biscay in the Fall of Seventeen.

But Aeolus was angry and loosed a tiny breeze,
Which crumpled up the ocean with overwhelming seas
Till each face was full of anguish, each countenance was green,
When we crossed the Bay of Biscay in the Fall of Seventeen.

Slum-gullion for breakfast, slum-gullion at noon,
With frequent interspersing of the ever-faithful prune.
These and other hardships would often intervene,
When we sailed the Bay of Biscay in the Fall of Seventeen.

84

But the sun is always shining in the pleasant land of France,
The women all are beautiful, you saw it at a glance.
The wine was effervescent, it has to be, I ween,
To tempt me 'cross old Biscay in the Fall of Seventeen.

When the struggle is concluded and victory is sure,
The foe must take some punishment most grievous to endure.
I'll offer this suggestion when the councillors convene—
They be made to cross old Biscay in some Fall of Seventeen.


We girls also thought it rough on shipboard with none but generals and their staffs. Only officers and ourselves were allowed above Deck 3. The men were below the waterline.

We landed on December 24 at Brest and were herded onto the wretched little French trains. Trains with no aisles, no plumbing—only unupholstered coops holding twelve of us; but not as bad as those for "eight horses or forty men. . . ."

Eight of us were put into one coop with all our belongings and a carton of canned food. But no can opener. One of the nurses operated on the cans with a nail file. Our progress was very slow, and that December 25 was very different from an Indianapolis Christmas.

We had no idea where we were going, how long we would be on the train, or how long between stops. We did not soon forget Christmas Day on that train in wartorn France.

About three o'clock of the morning of December 26 the train stopped, and sleepy and disheveled we disembarked in two feet of snow. French civilians escorted various groups to their unheated quarters but no one seemed to mind the cold: we were so glad to be off that train. A little station bore the letters: CONTREXE-VILLE. Somehow the French provided us hot coffee.

Miss Pink Cathcart at Contrexeville, 1917: "My job to meet the wounded and write down all particulars. . . ."

Contrexeville was to be our home. It is in the Vosges Mountains about three hundred and fifty miles east and a little south of Paris. It was rated by the French as a famous watering spa. We soon found the water would remove everything but one's immortal soul. We had to drink it, cook with it, and bathe in it. That is, if the weather was not too cold, for we had no fires anywhere.

Gradually a few "stoves" the size of small coffee pots appeared among the chosen few. However, we had so much to do that we did not notice the cold. We continued to live on canned food until our own mess was established. This was poor comfort, as there was an order that we eat only supplies which came from the United States. The butter tasted as if it had walked over. I wrote home:—

". . . We are now assigned to our various quarters, the nurses at the back of one of the big resort hotels. I prefer (although it has no heat) a room where I can watch the French troops passing to and from the Front. A scene so tragic and dramatic that one can hardly understand. We are all working desperately to be ready for our first convoy of wounded. My job to meet them and write down all particulars . . . ."

# Afterward

Pink Cathcart's memoirs end before she met the darker side of war, the first convoys of wounded. She had left home with her distinguishing dark hair. She returned in eighteen months with white.

She then began a business career, in charge of the Travel Department of the Fletcher American Bank. Characteristically, she abandoned it to accompany "Mama" when she went to live in Europe to be with "Katie." She had long abandoned the thought of marrying: she knew that she could not bring herself to leave her family.

Lonelier years came when she survived the rest of her beloved family for twenty years. Her loyalty kept her at the "Old Corner" where she was born, scene of youthful crowds on the front porch, of happy Christmases, laughter and parlor games, and of the broken doll.

Her parents' aptitudes now showed: she began to read and study avidly the Classics that "Papa had brought home from the Store"—still in their shiny-black wrappers. Her gay letters to remaining friends did not admit her worry about failing sight.

She put all her cherished memories in careful order, neatly annotated the old sheet music and the faded photographs, wrapped in tissue the doll with the broken leg, and, beginning after she was eighty-five, wrote the foregoing pages of old and happy days: goodbye to her many friends. . . . She was interrupted in these memories during August of 1964.

# Index

# Index

Allen, Fredonia, 21
Allen, Dr. Horace R., 45-46
Alvey, E. H., 72
American National Bank, 35
Arnold, Matthew, 59
Atkins, Elias C., 29
Ayres, Frederick M., 38
Ayres, L. S., & Co., 35

Baker, Albert, 25
Baker, Florence (Mrs. Jacquelin S. Holliday), 35
Baker, Nancy (Mrs. Evans Woollen), 35, 51
Baker, Nell (Mrs. Chandler Dallam), 22
Baldwin, D. H., & Co., music store, 35
Baldwin, James H., 25
Band concerts, 53-55
Base Hospital No. 32, 82-87
Baseball Park, 72
Bates, Hervey, Jr., 25, 30, 38
Bates, Hervey, Sr., 30
Bates House, 30
"Bee Hive," 32
Besten & Langen, coats and furs, 43-44
Beveridge, Albert, 59-60
Bicycles, 42-43, 60-61
Bingham, Emily, 21
Bingham & Walk, jewelry store, 33
Blacherne, The, apartment house, 29
Black, James B., 25
Blind Asylum, 25, 27, 29
Bobbs-Merrill Company, 32
Bostock's Zoo, 37-38
Bostwick, Mary, 83
Bowen-Merrill Company, 32
Bradshaw, James M., 25
Brayton, Dr. Alembert, 68

Brennecke's Dancing School, 26, 35
Bright, Marie L., 21
Bronk, Belle, 21
Browning, Eliza, 35
Browning, Robert, 37
Browning and Sloan's drugstore, 37
Burckhardt, Dr. Louis, 73
Burford, Caroline (Mrs. Henry Rose Danner), 22
Buschmann & Co., grocery, 67
Butler, John M., 68

Cady, Charles W., 40
Cady, Mrs. Charles W., 28
Cathcart, Alice Morrison (Mrs. Robert W.), mother of Pink, 14, 32, 44-45, 65-66
Cathcart, Charlotte (Pink), birth, 14; society editor, 64-66; witness, 71-72; with Base Hospital 32, 82-87; death, 88
Cathcart, Kate (Mrs. Clarence Martindale), 23, 42-44, 60, 64
Cathcart, Robert Weir, father of Pink, 14, 25, 30, 32, 68-70
Cathcart, Cleland & Co., bookstore, 32, 68-70
Chaffee, Kate, 22
Chartrand, Father Joseph, 60
Christ Episcopal Church, 27, 28
Christian, Jessie (Mrs. Demarchus Brown), 60, 61
Christmas, 73-79
Circle Park Hotel, 28
Clark, Dr. Edmund D., 83
Claypool, Edward F., 28
Claypool Block, 31
Cleland, Harriet (Mrs. John A. Blair), 60
Cleland, John E., 59, 68-70
Clemmer, Dr. Fernandez O., 45

Coburn, Myla (Mrs. Frank Ferry Powell), 22
Coburn, William H., 25
Coffin, Annie (Mrs. David W.), 19, 31, 77
Coffin, David W., 19, 25, 77
Coffin, Florence, 19, 53, 77
Coffin, Minnie, 19, 53, 77
Combs, Dr. George W., 45
Compton, Dr. Joshua A., 45
Cones, Charles B., 25
Conner, William, 25
Contrexeville (France), 85, 86
Cornelius, Edward G., 29
Coughlen, William, 73
Cox, Jacob, 25
Craig's, candy store, 33
Culbertson, John W., 48
Cyclorama Building, 37-38

Davis, Frederick A. W., 56
Denison Hotel, 26, 35
Denny, Caleb S., 18, 25
Denny, Carrie, 18
Denny, George, 18
Denny, Mamie, 18
Dickson, George A., 35, 58
"Doctor's Row," 35, 45
Dollens, Blanche, 18
Dollens, Harry, 18
Duncan, John S., 68

Eastman, Dr. Joseph, 45
Eastman, Schleicher & Lee, carpets, etc., 35
Edson, Elmer, 14, 23
Edson, Hanford, 15, 23
Edson, Dr. Hanford A., 15, 25
Edson, Mrs. Hanford A., 34
Eldridge, Mrs. Edward H., 15
Electric lighting, 39-40
English, William H., 28
English's Opera House, 28, 58
Entertainment, 12, 53-62
Erwin, Daniel P., 29

Fahnley, Frederick, 28
Fair Bank Park, 55

Fairbanks, Adelaide, 22
Fairview Park, 55
Fertig, Katrina, 72
Fesler, Mrs. Caroline Marmon, 40
Finch, Maria M. (Mrs. H. Byron), 49, 76
Finlay, Georgia, 83
First Baptist Church, 25
First Presbyterian Church, 25
Fishback, Robert, 60, 61
Fishback, William P., 50-60, 61, 62, 68, 70
Fisher, Carl, 26, 42
Fletcher, Albert, 79
Fletcher, Allen M., 29
Fletcher, Calvin, 79
Fletcher, Ingram, 79
Fletcher, Julia (Mrs. J. Alfred Barnard), 22
Fletcher, Louisa (Mrs. Willard Connelly), 22
Fletcher, S. A., & Co., bank, 33-34
Fletcher, Samuel, 73
Fletcher, Stoughton J., 34
Flower Mission Fair, 60
Foster, Chapin, 25
Fourth Presbyterian Church, 24, 27, 57
Frost, Geraldine, 83
Fugate, Fannie (Mrs. G. Harold Noyes), 60, 61
Fugate, James L., 25
Fulton, Albert, 14, 15, 23
Fulton, Fred, 15, 23
Fulton, Harmon H., 15
Fulton, Robert, 15, 25

Gall, Albert, carpet and wall paper store, 35
German House, 55
Girls' Classical School, 20-22
Godown, John M., 18
Godown, Kate, 19
Godown, Lottie, 19
Godown, Mary, 19
Grace Episcopal Church, 9, 51

Gramling, P., & Son, tailors, 35
Grand Opera House, 26, 35, 58
Graydon, Andrew, 30
Griffiths, John L., 60, 62, 68
Groceries, 67-68

Haerle, George, 32
Haerle, William, women's accessories store, 32
Hanna, Hugh H., 25
Harris, Addison C., 29
Harrison, Alfred, 29
Harrison, Benjamin, 32
Harry, Joseph, 48
Harvey, Dr. T. B., 45
Hasty, Dr. George, 45
Haueisen, Robert, 73
Haueisen, William, 73
Hawkins, Roscoe O., 73
Hays, Dr. Franklin W., 25, 29-30
Hays, Mrs. Franklin W., 29
Hendricks, Eliza, 69
Herod, Mary Beaty, 82, 83
Herod, William P., 29
Herron, Frederick P., 33
Herron, Frederick M., 15, 32-33
Herron, Walter, 15-16
Heywood, Florence, 22
Hodges, Dr. Edward F., 28
Holliday, John H., 29
Holliday, W. J., 29
Hollweg, Louis, 29
Hornbrook, Henry H., 73
Howland, Caroline, 62
Howland, John D., 73
Howland, Louis, 62
Hubbard, William H., 31
Hughes, Elizabeth, 21
Hunter, Ellis, 42
Hunter, Winifred, 42
Hurty, Dr. John N., 25, 26

Indiana Banking Co., 35
Indiana State Fair, 49-50
Indianapolis High School, 25
Indianapolis Light and Power Co., 40

Indianapolis Literary Club, 59-60
Indianapolis Public Library, 26, 51

Jameson, Dr. Henry, 45
Jameson, Dr. Patrick H., 45
Jenckes, Rev. Joseph S., Jr., 25
Johnson, Romeo, 53
Johnston, John, 25
Jones, Aquilla, 19
Jones, Charlotte, 19
Jones, Florence, 19
Jones, Robert, 19
Jordan, Arthur, 29
Journal Building, 40

King, Mrs. Abby, 29
Kitchen, Dr. John M., 25
Knippenberg, Henry, 29
Kothe, William, 73
Krauss, Charles, 25
Krauss, Paul, haberdashery, 26, 34
Krull, Frederic (Fritz), 55
Kuhn, A. C., grocery, 67
Kuhn, August M., 73

Landers, Dwight, 19
Landers, Franklin, 19, 25
Landers, Julia, 19
Landers, Pearl, 19
Landers, Thomas, 19
Laurie, William, & Co., dry goods, 44-45
Leckner, Max, 25
Lieber, Carl, 31
Lieber H., & Co., 31
Lieber, Herman, 31
Lieber, Otto, 31
Lieber, Robert, 31
Lighting, gas and electric, 39-40
Lilly, Col. Eli, 29, 73, 82
Lilly, Eli, and Co., 48
Lilly, J. K., 25, 68, 70, 73, 82
Lincoln, Abraham, 30
Literary clubs, 58, 59-60
Lodge, Caleb Newell, 14, 18, 23
Lodge, James I., 25

Lowe, Mrs. George, 18

McCulloch, Dr. Carleton, 59, 83, 84-85
McCulloch, David, 59
McCulloch, Oscar, 68
McDonald, Joseph E., 25
McIntosh, Andrew J., 73
McMurray, Dr. A. S., 45
Maennerchor, 55
Mansfield, Richard, 62
Mansur, Isaiah, 28
Marcy, William T., 48
Marmon, Daniel W., 39-40
Martin, Florence J., 82
Martindale, Elijah B., Jr., 16
Martindale, Elijah B., Sr., 16, 29, 73
Martindale, Emma, 16
Martindale, Lynn, 62
Mason, Augustus L., 62
Maxwell, Dr. Allison, 45
Mayer, Charles, 29, 41
Mayer, Ferdinand L., 41, 65, 66
Mayer, Charles, & Co., 35, 40-41, 65
Mayhew, James N., 48
Mayo, Edward H., 25
Meigs, Charles D., 18, 25, 32
Merchants National Bank, 35
Meridian Street Methodist Church, 16, 28
Merrill, Charles, 32
Merrill, Col. Samuel, 31-32
Merrill, Hubbard and Co., 31-32
Metzger, Alexander, 73
Meyer, Charles F., & Brother, tobacco store, 32
Morris, Gen. Thomas A., 68
Morrison, Frank, 51
Morrison, Dr. Frank, 82
Morrison, John I., 28, 73
Morrison, William H., 25, 28, 40
Morton, Mrs. (Dr.) Pauline, 22
Moses, Hannah E., 26, 48
Moses, Lucius W., 26

Murphy, John H., 25

New, Harry S., 73
New, John C., 25, 68
New York Store, 35
Nicholas, Anna, 69

Oliver, Dr. John, 82, 83

Perrin, Eleanor Bates, 35
Perrin, John, 35
Perry, Charles C., 39-40
Perry, James, 40
Perry, Joseph R., 18
Perry, Norman, 40
Pfaff, Dr. O. G., 25, 82
Pfaff, Mrs. O. G., 28, 72
Picnics, 56-57
Pierce, Henry D., 29
Plymouth Congregational Church, 28
Pomroy's drugstore, 25
Porter, Albert G., 73
Potts, Alfred L., 62
Powers, J. T., grocery, 67
Pratt, Louis, 17
Pratt, Ruth, 17
Pyle House, 28

Railsback, Charles, grocery, 67-68
Ransdell, Col. Daniel M., 73
Ransdell, Mamie (Mrs. Richard Warner), 22, 60
Raub, Edward, 60
Rauch, John, 73
Reed, Rev. Myron W., 60, 68
Reisner, George A., Jr., 73
Reisner, George A., Sr., 73
Rhodes, Charles, 18
Rhodes, Luella (Pudge), 18
Rhodes, William A., 18
Rhodes, William E., 18
Rich, Marie, 60
Richards, Bessie, 16
Richards, Edward, 16
Richards, Nellie, 15-16

Richards, Major William J., 25
Riley, James Whitcomb, 60, 62, 68
Roache, Addison L., 68
Robbins, Corinna, 21
Rorison, Brainard, 29
Ross, Dr. David, 82
Ruddell, Almus, 60, 61
Ruddell, Frank, 60, 61
Ruddell, Mrs. James H., 60-61

Schmidt, Alvin, 55
Schonacker, Isabella, 35
Schurmann, Henry, 25
Second Presbyterian Church, 25
Sentinel Building, 28
Severin, Henry, 29
Sewall, May Wright, 20-23
Sewall, Theodore L., 20-22
Sloan, George W., 29, 37
Smith, Albert, 16, 23
Smith, Charles W., 16, 68
Smith, Grace, 16-17, 23
Smith, Kate, 16
Smith, Margaret, 16
Spann, John M., 79
Spann, John S., 25, 79
Spann, Thomas, 79
State Fair, 49-50
Steele, Theodore C., 25
Steffen, Gertrude, 83
Steinberg, Mayer, 48
Stillson, Dr. Joseph, 25
Streetcars, 9, 24, 50-53
Sullivan, Miss _____, 33
Sullivan, Katherine (Mrs. John E.
    Hollett, Sr.), 22
Sullivan, Thomas L., 73

Taggart, Thomas, 73
Talbott, Henry M., 35, 58
Talbott, Will, 62
Tarkington, Booth, 25, 53
Tarkington, John S., 25
Theaters, 58-59
Third Ward School, 28
Thompson, Daniel W., 48

Thompson, James L., 48
Todd, Dr. Luther L., 45
Tomlinson, Dr. J. M., 45
Transfer Car, 9, 52
Tucker, Hannibal S., glove store,
    33

University Park, 25, 28

Vajen, John H., 28
Vajen Block, 26, 35
Van Camp, Dolly (Mrs. John T.
    Martindale), 22
Vernon, Dr. G. W., 45

Walk, Julius C., & Son, 33
Walker, Camilla, 15
Walker, Charles, 33
Walker, Dr. Isaac, 25-26
Walker, Dr. John C., 25-26
Walker, Lewis C., 15, 25
Walker, Mrs. Lewis C., 15-16
Wallick, John F., 29
Walling, Willoughby, 28
Wasson, H. P., & Co., 32
Wasson, Hiram P., 32
Watterson, Minnie, 40
Wehrman, Dr. Ernest A., 45
Wesley Chapel, 28
Whallon, Arthur, 18
Whallon, Rev. Edward P., 18
Whallon, Thomas, 18, 23
Whallon, Walter, 18
When Band, 11, 12, 28, 53
Wiggins, Joseph P., 29
Wildman, James A., 25
Winter, Ferdinand, 25
Wocher, _____, 34
Wocher, Frank, 71, 72
Wood, Bert, 23
Woollen, Mrs. W. W., 69
Wulsin, Clarence, 29, 35
Wulsin, Lucien, 35
Wynne, Thomas A., 40

Yandes, George, 68
Yandes, Simon, 36, 68

GREENVILLE COLLEGE LIBRARY

3 4511 00172 1022

977.252 C28

Cathcart, Charlotte, 1877-
1964.

Indianapolis from our old
corner